About the ___

Tony was born in Nottingham in 1952. In his twenties the seeds were sown for his love affair with Greece during a holiday on the island of Skiathos. Since then he has visited many of the islands of the Ionian and Aegean seas, as well as the mainland of Greece.

His heart though lies on the small, unspoilt islands of the Aegean. When in 2006, he had the opportunity of retiring from his business consultancy, he and his partner Carol chose Thassos as their base as UK ex-pats, selecting to live on the outskirts of Thassos Town, known locally as Limenas.

As an author of business books, Tony had been aware after his many years travelling within Greece that what was lacking for the holidaymaker and general traveller was a comprehensive, honest and accurate guide to each island in an easy to read book.

In 2006 he wrote a book on his adopted island home of Thassos, which has become a benchmark for holiday guides, selling extensively in Europe and the United States.

And so, in 2007 he decided to write this second book, on the island of Kos adding a third a year later on Santorini. His latest guide first published in 2013 is on the island of Rhodes. He hopes that in the years to come, his continuing travels will allow him to write guides for more of the Greek islands that he loves.

Opposite: A mosaic floor from the Asklepion on Kos, portraying Asklepius (*middle figure*) arriving by boat on Kos, with Hippocrates seated on the left. (*Archaeological Museum, Kos Town*)

A-Z Guide to

Kos

including Nisyros and Bodrum

Tony Oswin

Contents:
The island, its history, what to see, where to go, eating out,
entertainment, the best beaches, travel information and a host
of tips and hints for the holidaymaker and traveller.

2016 Edition

Published January 2016 by arima publishing
www.arimapublishing.com
9th edition

ISBN: 978 1 84549 673 9

Printed and bound in the United Kingdom

Typeset in Arial 12/14

DISCLAIMER
The contents of these materials are for general guidance only and are not
intended to apply in specific circumstances. As such, the contents of these
materials should not be relied on for the purpose of deciding to do, or
omitting to do anything, and you should always seek independent advice in
relation to any particular question or requirement you might have. Any
opinions set out in these materials are those of the author only, and unless
expressly stated otherwise, are not the opinions of the publisher. To the
fullest extent permitted by law, the publisher and Tony Oswin expressly
disclaims any and all liability and responsibility to any person, in respect of
the consequences of anything done, or omitted to be done, in reliance on
the contents of these materials.

arima publishing, ASK House, Northgate Avenue
Bury St. Edmonds, Suffolk IP32 6BB
t: (+44) 01284 700321

www.arimapublishing.com

To Carol....for all her loving support

Foreword

I have been visiting Greece for over thirty years and during that time I have fallen in love with the country, its people and most of all the Greek approach to life.

However, during my travels I always found it difficult to obtain island specific guide books, written in English and containing up to the minute information and advice. Too many times, I returned home from a visit to Greece, only to talk to someone who advised me of something to do or see that I had been unaware of.

After moving to Greece in 2006, I realised that I now had the time and opportunity to fulfil that need, starting with a guide book on my adopted home island of Thassos. This, my second book in the series, is aimed at helping you to get the most out of your time on the cosmopolitan island of Kos. I hope that you will find it helpful and informative, both in planning your holiday and during your stay.

Occasionally I have been asked why there are no photographs in the book? When I first set out to write my travel guides, one major objective was to make sure the books were accurate and with the latest information at an affordable price. To achieve this, the publication process I chose was POD (*Print on Demand*), whereby each book is printed at the time of order, from a manuscript that is regularly updated. However, one drawback of POD is that at present, the addition of colour photographs adds considerably to the cost of each book.

As is the practice with books containing photographs, if they are to be offered at a reasonable price, they are printed in bulk to reduce the unit cost. This inevitably means that at these quantities, the book can be significantly out of date when purchased.

I hope you therefore agree that my decision to move all the media to the supporting website, so as to offer you both the highest quality and ensure the accuracy of island information, was the correct one.

As both official and local organisations have a habit of not releasing tourist related news, or information on tourist events until a few days before they start, I strongly recommend that you visit the website regularly whilst on the island. The latest news from the island is updated throughout each day to keep you constantly informed.

I wish you a wonderful 2016 holiday,

Tony Oswin

Our website can be found at:-

www.atoz-guides.com

(*your password can be found on the 'Acknowledgements' page at the back of this book*)

Our email address is:-

info@atoz-guides.com

A to Z Travel Club

Unique amongst travel guides, the 'A to Z' guides are designed in two parts. The printed book, which contains all the information you need on your travels around the island and the 'A to Z' website, which offers a wealth of supporting information. The website also allows us to bring you the very latest tourist news from the island, special 'members' offers and more high quality photographs and videos than with any other travel guide, including over 50 photographs, panoramas, videos and webcams on the island.

All this is totally free to you and is accessed via a member's password. You will find your member password at the bottom of the 'Acknowledgements' page at the back of this book.

To access the full member benefits of the website, place your cursor over the 'Travel Club' button at the top of any website page. Next move your cursor down over 'Travel Club Kos' and a further drop down menu appears, then place your cursor over the desired page and click:-

Kos News - Tourist news updated throughout each day

Holiday Advice - A wide range of holiday related advice

Discounts & Offers - Holiday ideas and money saving offers

Kos 2D Gallery - Over 45 high quality photographs and videos

Kos Weather - Real-time weather and an 8 day forecast

Kos Travel Info - Flight information, money matters etc.

Kos Maps & Panoramas - Print-off maps and panoramas

Kos Links - Webcams and a wide range of Kos websites

Contents

Kos

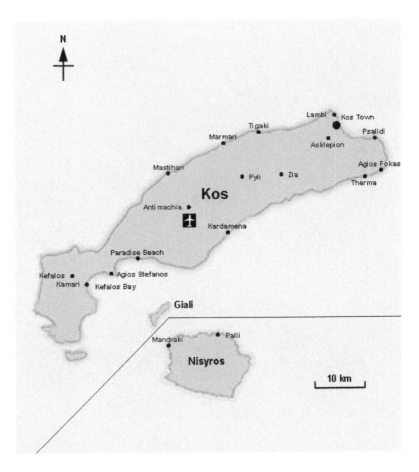

Due to the small size of the book, we are unable to include a more detailed map. However, if you visit our website there are basic and detailed maps of the island to download and print off. Alternatively there are free maps available from most car hire companies and many other businesses once you are on the island.

The golden island of Kos

Kos or Cos (*Greek - Κως*) is an island in the Dodecanese chain, next to the Gulf of Kerme and only 23 km from Bodrum on the coast of Turkey. The island has an area of 290 sq km and measures approximately 45 km long by between 2 and 11 km wide. The north of the island is composed of fertile plains, whilst the south offers the visitor picturesque highlands, with Mount Dikaio being the highest peak at 843 metres.

The resident population (*Koans*) was 30,502 at the last census. In the summer months, Kos attracts around 700,000 visitors, with the UK contributing approximately 220,000 to this figure. Kos Town and Kardamena are the two main resorts, but hotels and apartments have sprung up behind most beaches, with those along the flat far northern coastline, being more isolated from the hustle and bustle of the larger resorts.

Kos is one of the main European holiday destinations in the Aegean Sea. Sadly though, tourism has had a detrimental effect on the architecture and environment. It has also been a major factor in the diminishing role of traditional Greek culture on the island.

The island lies in the centre of the Dodecanese chain, derived from the Greek word for *twelve islands*, which since additions after the Second World War, now comprises fourteen islands. These are Kos, Rhodes, Symi, Megisiti, Lipsoi, Telos, Astypalia, Kalymnos, Karpathos, Kasos, Leros, Nisyros, Patmos and Halki.

Kos lies southeast of mainland Greece and northwest of Rhodes. It is the third largest of the Dodecanese after Rhodes and Karpathos and is a major province within the Dodecanese Prefecture. Kos is the administrative capital of Nisyros, Giali, Pergoussa, Kandeliousa,

Pahia and Strongyli.

Kos offers the visitor both the opportunity to relax on the many beautiful beaches, as well as the chance to explore the island's fascinating history at the many archaeological sites, both in Kos Town and around the island. This broad appeal means that Kos has become one of the prime destinations for a Greek island holiday and bestows on the island a busy cosmopolitan feel.

Geology

The island was formed when, as one of a range of peaks on a single island, it became separated by seismic upheavals and major marine subsidence. The fragmentation of this original island also created Kalymnos and Kappari, as well as the volcanic island of Nisyros and other neighbouring islands. The former two are now divided by an underwater chasm 40 fathoms deep.

There are a wide variety of rocks on Kos that are related to its geological formation. Prominent among these are the Quaternary layers, in which the fossil remains of mammals such as prehistoric examples of hippopotami, horses and elephants have been found. This confirms that in the distant past, the island was joined to the mainland of what is now Turkey.

The island of Kos is part of one of the largest volcanic calderas in Europe. Around 140,000 years ago the south-western part of Kos was blown into the air by the huge eruption that was many times greater than the 1,627 B.C. catastrophic eruption of Santorini. As you travel through the central part of the island you will see the vast deposits of pumice and pyroclastic flows that give this region a moon-like and desolate panorama. The south-western part of Kos, the Kefalos peninsula, is dominated by huge extinct volcanic domes. The islands of Nisyros, Strongyli and Giali are the present day active remnants of this ancient volcano.

History

Prehistoric to Classical period

Kos has been known by many names in antiquity, *Karis, Meropis* and *Kinnis* being three, with Plini the Elder (*23 - 79 A.D.*) calling the island *Nimphea* and who commentated on its magnificent wine. Kos is known to have been inhabited from the early Bronze Age (*2,900-2,100 B.C.*), as the prehistoric tombs and artefacts found in Asklupi and the White Stone cave testify (see *page 58*). The tribes Leleges and Carians, are mentioned as some of the first to colonise the island. Archaeological finds include artefacts from the late Bronze Age (*1600 - 1150 B.C.*), including many of Mycenaean origin. The Phoenicians invaded and settled on the island, as did the Achaeans (*a collective name for the early Greek tribes*).

In the Iliad, Homer tells of Kos along with the islands of Nisyros, Kalymnos, Karpathos and Kassos as taking part in the Trojan War, sending Pheidippos and Antiphos, sons of King Thessalos and thirty ships of warriors to join the Greek army. The Dorians, who were one of the three initial tribes by which the ancient Greeks classified themselves, invaded Kos in the 11th century B.C. During the 7th century B.C. the island became a member of the *Doric Hexapolis*, a league of six city-states which included Halicarnassus (*modern day Bodrum*), Knidus in Turkey, and Lalyssos, Lindos and Kameiros on Rhodes. The prime objective of the league was to combine the forces of the six to offer mutual protection.

In the 5th century B.C., the island of Kos was occupied by the Persians and was forced to participate as allies in the Battle of Salamis (*480 B.C.*), which saw the navy of the Greek city-states triumph over that of the Persians. Following the victory, Kos was liberated by the Greeks and joined the Athenian League which was also known as the Delian League.

The league was comprised of Greek city-states and those who, like the Greeks, saw both the Persian Empire and others as a threat to free trade and independence in the Mediterranean. One prime objective of the league was to free cities dominated by rivals and to absorb them into the league. Many cities though had to join unwillingly being coerced by the league members, sometimes under threat of attack. Although the league was essentially democratic, they believed that the safety of the league and its objectives would be seriously compromised by city-states that sought to stay independent.

The wars against the Persians continued until 450 B.C., when the league achieved a decisive victory against them at Salamis, Cyprus (*not to be confused with the Battle of Salamis near Attica*). However, the aggressive posturing between Greece and Persia went on for many years after 450 B.C.

It was during the above period that the island's most famous son Hippocrates was born (*460 - circa 370 B.C*). Renowned as the "father of modern medicine", he studied and taught at the Asklepion on Kos (*see page 13*).

Just prior to the Hellenistic period, Kos saw the development of two capitals in the north of the island. One was *Meropis Kos* without a harbour and the other *Kos* with a good-sized harbour, the latter being established in 366 B.C. on the site of modern day Kos Town. Strabo, the famous Greek historian (*64 B.C. - 24 A.D.*) wrote about this latter city: "The city of Kos is not large, but it has been better constructed than all the others and looks beautiful to those passing by in their ships."

The early Hellenistic period

The Hellenistic period was the brightest period in Kos' history, with the island thriving both economically and culturally. Construction was prolific, seeing the addition of a large number of monumental public buildings, such as the sanctuaries of Hercules and Pandimou and Pondias Aphrodite, the market, the theatre, the gymnasium, the stadium, the temple of Dionysus and the acropolis.

Under Alexander the Great and later the Egyptian Ptolemies (*from 336 B.C.*) the town continued to develop as one of the great centres in the Aegean. Kos was not only rich in agricultural and livestock products, but also started developing its export trade in wine, olive oil, fruit, perfumes and wool.

The late Hellenistic period

Kos continued to prosper during the late Hellenistic period, with the construction of elegant buildings such as the conservatory and the Odeum, with their rich decoration, all demonstrating the luxury in which the Koans lived. The harbour of Kos was becoming one of the main centres of trade for the nearby islands and the wider Aegean region as a whole, a fact that increased the prosperity of the island and its people.

Flavius Josephus, a 1st century A.D. Jewish historian, quotes Strabo to the effect that a party was sent to Kos to fetch Queen Cleopatra's gold that was deposited on the island. King Herod of Judea also provided an annual stipend for the prize-winners of the athletic games on the island, and in gratitude, a statue was erected to his son Herod the Tetrarch in the city of Kos.

The Roman period

During the Roman period, Kos was absorbed into the eastern colony of the Roman Empire and in 82 B.C., was granted special privileges and relative autonomy. However, some of these privileges were withdrawn during the reign of the Emperor Augustus, initiating a decline in the prosperity of the island that was compounded by a major earthquake in 27 B.C. The island did recover again, in part due to the reputation of Hippocrates and the Asklepion. In the Christian Book of Acts, the island also features as an overnight stop during Saint Paul's journey to Jerusalem. Another important public figure of the 1st century A.D. was the Koan doctor Gaius Stertinius Xenophon, who became a courtier and physician to the Emperor Claudius in Rome. During the 5th and 6th centuries A.D., the construction of a number of early Christian basilicas, testifies to the island's continuing economic and artistic wealth.

The Byzantine period

During the first half of the 7th century, Kos became politically a part of the Byzantine Empire and despite the further adversity of earthquakes and incursions by pirates, mostly by Arabs, the island continued to be a major economic force within the Aegean. To confirm this, Efstathios, the Archbishop of Thessaloniki, wrote in the 12th century: "If Kos is not enough to satisfy your hunger, then neither is Egypt."

The Order of the Knights Hospitaller

The centuries that followed were marked by the presence of a variety of foreign conquerors. After a short occupation of the island by the Venetians, in 1314 they sold the island to the Knights Hospitaller of Rhodes (*also known as the Knights of St. John*). The order on the island had its own governors, who were imposed by the Council of the Knights of Rhodes and they closely controlled the island and its people. The 14th century saw the first attacks by the Turks. The Hospitallers successfully managed to repulse these on a number of occasions, largely due to the island's impressive fortifications. These included the main castle of Neratzia (*the common name being the Knight's Castle*) in Kos Town, the castle of Antimachia, which was unsuccessfully attacked in 1457, the castle of old Pyli and the castle of Kefalos. Even today, the repairs to the damage inflicted by the Turkish attacks on the two most important castles, those of Neratzia and Antimachia, are clearly visible.

Turkish rule

On 5th January 1523, the Knights Hospitaller finally surrendered and the Turks occupied the island. Rhodes and Kos, in contrast with other islands of the Dodecanese, suffered from heavier taxes imposed by the Turkish rulers. The Koans rallied round the Archbishop, who officiated under the direct jurisdiction of the Ecumenical Patriarchate, the supreme order of the Greek Orthodox Church, continually opposing Turkish rule on the island.

After the outbreak of the Greek Revolution in 1821, the Koans were made to pay dearly. On 11th July of that year, in retaliation for local support for the revolution, the Turks hung a group of priests under the historical plane tree of Hippocrates. According to a written testimony of the French traveller Pouqueville, the Turks also executed 900 local Christians. It was only after 1838 that the citizens of Kos were granted a few basic human and political rights.

The early 20th century

On 20th May 1912, the Italians invaded Kos and drove out the Turks. The inhabitants welcomed them as liberators, but soon found that their promise of a short occupation of the Dodecanese was a lie. After the treaty of Lausanne in the same year, the total Italian domination of the Dodecanese was consolidated and the inhabitants of the islands were considered Italian citizens with singular citizenship. Kos was governed as part of the Italian annexation of the Dodecanese, under the jurisdiction of Rhodes.

After the major earthquake of 23rd April 1933, the Italians rebuilt the devastated city of Kos. During the clearance work, Italian archaeologists revealed, excavated and repaired a large number of the ancient monuments in Kos Town. Sculptures from the Classical, Hellenistic and Roman periods, found during this work, are exhibited at the archaeological museum in Eleftherias Square.

In the early days of the Second World War, many volunteers from the island enlisted in the Dodecanese Regiment, which fought in the army of central Macedonia against the Axis forces.

After the Italian surrender in September 1943, a small British force landed on the island, welcomed by the Italians as a way of deterring a potential German assault. However, on 3rd October 1943, the island was attacked and taken by German forces. This signalled a new period of suppression and brutality against the islanders.

The post-war British administration

On 9th May 1945, after the signing of the protocol of Simi, which was the unconditional surrender of the Axis forces in the Dodecanese, British forces took full authority over Kos.

The local authorities were re-established, the schools that had been closed since 1938 reopened and the people were liberated from the suffering caused by the Italian and German occupations. Although the British coveted the Dodecanese, promoting the idea of autonomy under the British Crown, the decision of the Foreign Ministers of the Allied powers in Paris in June 1946, proposed an end to the British administration and the ceding of the islands back to Greece. This was finally approved at the peace conference in Paris in February 1947 and on 31st May the Greek armed forces replaced the British administration. The official celebration of the unification of the island with Greece was on 7th March 1948.

If nothing else, it is clear that throughout history, the Koans have proved to be highly skilled and resilient in the face of relentless adversity!

Greek historic periods (*B.C.*)

Archaic	800 - 480
Classical	480 - 323
Hellenistic	323 - 31

Hippocrates of Kos

Hippocrates of Kos (*460 - circa. 370 B.C.*), was an ancient Greek physician, considered as one of the most outstanding figures in the history of medicine. He is often referred to as the "father of modern medicine", in recognition of his lasting contributions to the science and as the founder of the Hippocratic School of Medicine. This intellectual school revolutionised medicine in ancient Greece, establishing it as a discipline and profession. It dismissed the traditional approach, which had derived cures from engaging in such methodologies as Theurgy (*the invoking of the gods to intervene*) and Philosophy.

These traditional approaches to illness tended to be highly superstitious and credited supernatural or divine forces with causing illness. Hippocrates separated the discipline of medicine from philosophy and religion, believing and arguing that disease was not a punishment inflicted by the gods, but rather the product of environmental factors, such as diet and lifestyle. Indeed, not a single mention of a supernatural illness can be found anywhere in the writings of Hippocrates. He did though work with many theories that were based on what today is known to be incorrect anatomy and physiology.

Around 357 B.C., soon after Hippocrates' death, building commenced on the Asklepion of Kos (*the ruins of which we see today*) and it was after that date that the cult of Asklepius assumed such a central role on the island.

The Hippocratic Oath

The Hippocratic Oath is an oath which to this day is pledged by graduating physicians. It requires them to swear an oath that they will uphold a number of professional and ethical standards. The original text set down by Hippocrates is as follows:

"I swear by Apollo Physician and Asklepius and Hygieia and Panaceia and all the gods and goddesses, making them my witnesses that I will fulfil according to my ability and judgment, this oath and covenant:

To hold him who has taught me this art, as equal to my parents and to live my life in partnership with him, and if he is in need of money to give him a share of mine, and to regard his offspring as equal to my brothers in male lineage and to teach them this art, if they desire to learn it, without fee and covenant; to give a share of precepts and oral instruction and all the other learning to my sons and to the sons of him who has instructed me and to pupils who have signed the covenant and have taken an oath according to the medical law, but no one else.

I will apply dietetic measures for the benefit of the sick according to my ability and judgment; I will keep them from harm and injustice.

I will neither give a deadly drug to anybody who asked for it, nor will I make a suggestion to this effect. Similarly I will not give to a woman an abortive remedy. In purity and holiness I will guard my life and my art.

I will not use the knife, not even on sufferers from stone, but will withdraw in favour of such men as are engaged in this work.

Whatever houses I may visit, I will come for the benefit of the sick, remaining free of all intentional injustice, of all mischief and in particular of sexual relations with both female and male persons, be they free or slaves.

What I may see or hear in the course of the treatment, or even outside of the treatment in regard to the life of men, which on no account one must spread abroad, I will keep to myself, holding such things shameful to be spoken about.

If I fulfil this oath and do not violate it, may it be granted to me to enjoy life and art, being honoured with fame among all men for all time to come; if I transgress it and swear falsely, may the opposite of all this be my lot."

Mythology

Prior to the twelve gods of Olympus gaining a popular following in Greece, the creator gods such as Gaia (*Earth*) and Uranus (*Sky*) were worshipped as the main deities, being part of the pantheon of gods known as the Giants, or Titans. The myths proclaim that a battle took place between the Giants and the Olympian gods, the latter led by Zeus the son of the Titan Chronos (*Time*). This is said to have shaken the very foundations of the universe and resulted in the final defeat of the Titans by the Olympians.

In the aftermath, the Giant known as Polivotis fled to seek refuge, followed by his nemesis Poseidon, the god of the sea. When Poseidon finally cornered Polivotis on Kos, he broke off a part of the island and hurled it at him, crushing the Giant and killing him. This, according to the myth is how the island of Nisyros was formed. Geologists have confirmed that Nisyros was originally part of Kos, but was separated in antiquity by a major earthquake.

The myth also states that other Titans such as Phoebus, Kios and his brother Kinnos, sought refuge on Kos and in fact Kinnos is said to have named it after himself, Kinnis.

In mythology the island is also linked with the most famous of all ancient Greek/Roman heroes, the invincible demi-god, Hercules.

Hercules

The leader of the twelve gods of Olympus was Zeus, armed with the lightning bolt; he was seen as all powerful. However, he had one fundamental weakness; he could not resist the attraction of beautiful mortal women. So when he saw the lovely Alcmene, the daughter of the King of Mycenae, he became infatuated. She was though married and so to achieve his objectives, Zeus took the form of her husband and Uncle Amphitryon, tricking her into making love to him. The union resulted in the birth of Hercules and therefore the son of a god and a mortal. The goddess Hera, the wife of Zeus, was forced to breast feed Hercules against her will, and this instilled in her a deep hatred for Hercules.

The twelve labours of Hercules

Years later, Hercules married Megara the oldest daughter of Creon, King of Thebes. Hera's continuing hatred of Hercules, finally drove her to hatch a plot to make Hercules suffer from a fit of madness, during which, he would kill both his wife Megara and his children.

The plan succeeded and when Hercules regained his sanity and realised what he had done, he was mortified. He proceeded to Delphi to ask the oracle how he could atone for his crime. The oracle announced that the only path to atonement was to serve his cousin Eurystheus, the King of Tyrins and do anything the king demanded of him. Hera, hearing of this, saw her opportunity to continue her scheming to destroy Hercules.

When Hercules arrived at Tyrins, his cousin now controlled by Hera, decreed that Hercules would have to perform 12 perilous labours. These labours were to slay the *Nemean Lion* and bring back its fur, slay the *Lernaean Hydra*, trap the *Ceryneian Hind*, catch the *Erymanthian Boar*, clean the *Augean stables* in a single day, slay the *Stymphalian Birds*, capture the *Cretan Bull*, steal the *Mares of Diomedes*, obtain the *Girdle of Hippolyte*, seize the *Cows of Geryon*, take the *Apples of the Hesperides* and snatch *Cerberus*, the guardian dog of Hades and bring him back to the world of the living.

Hera had set the labours to be so difficult and dangerous that they seemed impossible. Fortunately, Hercules had the help of Hermes and Athena, sympathetic deities who intervened when the situation became dire. Hercules successfully completed all the labours, much to the aggravation of Hera and in so doing proved without a doubt, that he was Greece's greatest hero.

His struggles made Hercules the perfect embodiment of an idea the Greeks called *pathos*, the experience of virtuous struggle and suffering which would lead to fame and, in Hercules' case, immortality.

Hercules at Troy

Having accomplished all twelve labours, Hercules was impelled to undertake others of lesser importance but none the less, they proved just as perilous.

King Laomedon of Troy called on Hercules to help destroy a sea monster that had been sent by the god Poseidon to attack Troy. It had been foretold that Poseidon would be appeased if Laomedon offered his daughter, Hesione, as bride to the monster. However, as this would result in the death of his daughter, Laomedon could not bring himself to comply.

Therefore King Laomedon called on Hercules and promised that if he were to slay the monster, his prize would be the magnificent royal horses that Zeus had given to the king. Hercules did indeed slay the monster and thus saved Hesione, but the king reneged on his promise. Hercules, enraged, gathered together a band of warriors and attacked Troy, killing the king and plundering his kingdom.

Hercules on Kos

Hercules left Troy with his warrior companions in six ships heavily laden with Trojan treasure, but during the voyage the ships were caught in a great storm. Once again, it was Hera's unbridled hatred for Hercules that had provoked her to initiate the storm, determined that this time, he would be killed.

Five of the six ships sank, with everyone on board being lost, but Hercules' ship survived and with his remaining crew he managed to land on Kos, at what today is known as Cape Gourniatis.

Once on the island, Hercules met a young shepherd called Antagoras and demanded food from him. The shepherd, offended by this arrogant order and being physically strong himself, refused. This outraged Hercules, who attacked the young shepherd and they fought for a long time with no man gaining the upper hand. Antagoras came from Antimachidon (*modern day Antimachia*) and

17

hearing of the conflict, the citizens of Antimachidon came to Antagoras' aid and a ferocious battle ensued.

Outnumbered, Hercules and his companions managed to escape and sought protection in the house of a Thracian woman, who helped them disguise themselves and flee into the mountains. There, in a town called Phixioton near present day Pyli, the inhabitants welcomed Hercules and his companions and apologised for the conduct of the people of Antimachidon. To try to compensate for the wrong done to Hercules, the people of Phixioton asked him to become their king, Hercules agreed and as king declared war on Antimachidon.

Antimachidon was ruled by King Eurypylus, son of the god Poseidon. Hercules and Eurypylus were therefore evenly matched, both being sons of gods. Eventually though, Hercules managed to overcome and kill Eurypylus. The new King of Antimachidon, Halkonas, ended the war and to appease Hercules, gave his sister Halkiopi's hand in marriage. In time Halkiopi gave birth to their son Thessalos, who later became the King of Kos and Nisyros.

On his death and by virtue of his spectacular achievements, Hercules was given a home with the gods on Mount Olympus and a goddess for a wife. However, being the offspring of a mortal as well as a god, his mortal spirit was sent to the Underworld. As a ghost, his spirit is said to eternally roam the Elysian Fields, in the company of the other great heroes.

Culture

For those who have not visited Greece before, how can I explain the Greek people and their culture? It could be said that their way of life reflects many of the positive attributes of the UK in the not so distant past. These include a greater reliance and respect within the community for the family as well as the individual, a belief that the quality of life is more important than the quantity and a stronger self-reliance, rather than an increasing dependence on the state.

All I will say is that I find the Greek islanders honest, sincere and extremely friendly and one of my greatest hopes is that the ever-increasing exposure to the tourist trade does not devalue, or corrupt these virtues.

You will find that, as in many Mediterranean countries, much of the day-to-day activities start very early, stop at lunchtime and reconvene early evening, continuing late into the night. So expect many of the shops and other services to be closed for a few hours in the afternoon. Remember the old adage "only mad dogs and Englishmen go out in the midday sun". I can confirm though there are no mad dogs, you will see a few that appear to be stray, but the majority have owners who let them out to wander free during the day. All in my experience are very friendly and pose no risk.

During your stay, one of the simplest ways of saying thank you (*Efkaristo*) is to take time to learn a few basic Greek words and phrases. I can assure you that even though the majority of Koans in the main tourist areas speak at least a little English, your attempt to speak their language, if only a few words, will be much appreciated. To that end, I have added a glossary of frequently used Greek words and phrases at the back of the book.

Beyond the tourist

With the first drops of rain another summer season comes to a close. The days get shorter and the sunsets are a deeper red and purple. The Meltemi winds (*the Aegean equivalent of the French Mistral*) appear more strongly in the evenings. There is a fresher feel in the air; reminding all on the island that winter is approaching.

The warm sunny weather continues for the whole of September and well into October. The first fallen leaves bring a new urgency, the tourists may be leaving, but this is a busy time for the islanders.

Many of the locals have two separate lives, the first during the holiday season, working in one of the many service industries dedicated to the tourist industry. Then, once the tourists have left, another that is more reminiscent of the past life on the island, which includes amongst others, working in agriculture, fishing and community services.

Winters on Kos are mild, with temperatures dropping to around 10°C during January and February. Showers can be expected between October and May, with December tending to be the wettest month, rainfall decreases dramatically after March. The sun continues to shine during the winter, with Kos still receiving roughly 4 to 5 hours a day during this time.

Olive picking

The olive picking season usually starts in early November. The hills and mountains all around the island of Kos come alive with the sights and sounds of families collecting the olives, as they have done for generations. The men beat the olives down from the trees using long sticks (*or, more often nowadays, an electric beater*), whilst the women and children pick them up off large nets that are spread under the olive trees. When the olives have been gathered, those not destined for eating whole, are taken to the olive press, where they are pressed to extract the olive oil.

The first oil of the season is the best and is used for salads, etc., whilst the old oil from last year is reserved for frying, or for lighting the icon lamps in the church.

Only in mid-December can the people of Kos slow down and start preparing for Christmas.

Cultural events

Below is a list of some of the cultural events during the summer months. However, news on such attractions as festivals, cultural events and concerts, will be posted on the 'Rhodes News' page on our website throughout the season.

The Hippocratia

The most important event, called the Hippocratia, runs from July to September. This festival includes classical and contemporary music concerts, theatrical works, folklore, art exhibitions, sculpture and photographic exhibitions. Also included are traditional dance and song shows, special educational and entertainment events for children, and last but not least, and where it gets its name, a theatrical reading of the Hippocratic Oath.

The Dikea

The Dikea is organized by the Municipality of Dikeos during July and August. This festival includes concerts, theatrical performances, traditional dances, attractions for children and a variety of sporting events.

The Heraclia

The Heraclia, organized by the Municipality of Iraklidon, takes place during the months of July and August. This festival includes concerts, theatrical performances, traditional music and dance, and photographic exhibitions.

Religious celebrations and customs

Easter to Greeks is the most important religious time of the year and as in other countries a celebration of Spring. Easter doesn't always fall on the same date as in most countries, as the Greek Orthodox Church uses the ancient Julian calendar, rather than the more usual Gregorian calendar. In 2016, Orthodox Easter Sunday falls on 1st May.

At Easter in Greece, people leave the cities to spend the holiday in the countryside, many in their ancestral villages.

Many other religious events are continued, or have been revived, not only in respect for the history and religious beliefs of the islanders, but also as attractions for the tourists who visit Kos.

The feast of Agios Georgios is held on 23rd April in Pyli, when horse races are held and in Asfendiou and the local inhabitants prepare mezes and have a picnic in the surrounding countryside.

On 29th June the feast of the Holy Spirit is held in Antimachia.

In Antimachia and Kardamena the *Niamero* begins on the feast of the Transfiguration of Christ the Saviour. This event relates to fulfilling a promise to the Virgin Mary that was made at a difficult moment in one's life. Those taking part attend confession in the morning and in the evening gather to recite various hymns in front of the Virgin's icon. The feast starts on the evening of the Transfiguration on 6th August after vespers and finishes on the eve of the Feast of the Virgin (*Dormition*) on 14th August before vespers.

One of the most important dates in the Greek Orthodox religious calendar is the Feast of the Virgin on the 15th August. In Kefalos, the local farmers prepare boiled goat and serve this with rice to all that attend during the feast and on the same day the feast of the Apostles is held in Antimachia.

The feast of Agios Ioannis is celebrated on 28th August in Mastihari, with the birthday of the Virgin Mary being celebrated on 8th September in Kardamena and 28th August in Agios Ioannis.

The Presentation of the Virgin in the Temple is celebrated on 21st November in Kefalos and Agios Dimitrios and on 26th October in Asfendiou.

Festivals

The Fanos

This tradition coincides with the summer solstice on 21st June, which historically was considered one of the most auspicious dates in the annual cycle. For this reason, the ancient Koans undertook various religious and ceremonial rights at this time, the Fanos being one. Today, on the evening of the 21st, as the sun goes down, fires are lit in the streets and in front of each house. The old and the young have to jump up and down three times. Every effort is made to ensure that the jumps are taken when the flames are at their most intense, as the ancient belief is that by jumping higher than the highest flames, the magical properties of the flame will be transferred to the participant and thus robbing the fire of its strength.

The Klidona

Preparations for this fortune telling custom begin on the eve of the feast of Agios Ioannis. The Klidona requires that all the single girls of the village, who are dressed in traditional costume, offer in silence a water jug to the other members of the village. They in turn, are required to throw a personal item such as a ring, earring, or brooch into the jug.

After passing amongst all present, the girls remove the items one by one, whilst reciting traditional incantations. These verses are supposed to reveal the fate of the girl in relation to each item. The evening celebrations continue with song and dance around bonfires, which are lit with May Day wreathes and from which it derives its name of Fire Night.

In the first week of August, a wine festival is held in Mastihari, while during the first half of the same month, there is a fish festival and honey festival in Kefalos and Antimachia respectively. During the first ten days of October, a fish festival is also held in Kardamena.

Many customs are practiced during August. The first six days of August in Greece are known as Drimes and which, dependent on the area of the Greece, have their own traditional customs. Three such local customs on Kos are that you should not swim in the sea during the Drimes, or you risk having your hair fall out, black figs and grapes are not to be eaten and clothes should not be washed.

The Minalogia begins on the first day of August. This custom is concerned with the forecasting the weather for the year to come. It is traditionally believed that the 1st - 12th of August correspond to the twelve months of the year. Thus the weather on these days, predicts the weather to be expected throughout the corresponding months to come.

The Festival of the Holy Spirit

May 31st, a major festival and bank holiday across Greece. In western Christianity it is known as Pentecost.

The Dormition

August 15th, the day celebrating the Virgin Mary's ascension into heaven, is the second most important day on the Eastern Orthodox calendar. Throughout Greece, the Feast of the Dormition is celebrated in a variety of ways. The religiously devout attend church services and undertake pilgrimages, while others spend the day dining and dancing with family and friends or enjoying regional traditions.

New Year

In 313 A.D. the 1st September was established as the beginning of the religious year by the Greek Orthodox Church and that day continues to be celebrated on Kos as New Year's Day. One custom at this time requires women and children to hug the enormous trunk of Hippocrates' Plane Tree in Kos Town, whilst reciting verses that wish for the tree to grant them some of its power and some years from its own life.

Local products

Crafts

The islanders' of Kos are known for their production of fine porcelain, ceramics and jewellery.

Honey

Honey is produced on the island, with the main centre of apiculture in the villages of Kefalos and Antimachia. Look out for the brightly coloured beehives lining the roads and fields. In the villages, visitors are welcome to taste the honey and maybe buy some to take home.

Olives

Those farmed on Kos are low tree varieties that crop heavily and give both high quality light coloured oil and delicious edible black olives. However, the bags of local olives that can be purchased in the supermarkets can be quite salty for some people's taste, so it may be better opting for the variety in jars.

Weaving

Traditional weaving is centred in the villages of Antimachia and Asfendiou.

Wine

The quality of Kos wines was celebrated by many famous ancient writers, who commented on their excellence and individuality. However, with the Roman domination of the Mediterranean, the centre of wine production shifted from the north and central to the southern Aegean, and finally away from Greece altogether.

Wine is still produced on the island, but the number of vineyards has radically decreased since antiquity, which means that wine is no-longer a major product of Kos.

Local animals

Birds

There is a wide variety of bird life on the island, including the Common Sparrow, which you will find are very tame, a wide variety of owls (*their calls are a familiar sound during the night*) and an impressive number of birds of prey. Here are just a few of the many species you may see, Buzzard, Kestrel, Little Ringed Plover, Redshank, Greenshank, Little Stint, Yellow-legged Gull, Alpine Swift, Pallid Swift, Common Swift, Kingfisher, Bee-eater, Crested Lark, Flycatcher, Wood Warbler, Lesser Whitethroat, Sardinian Warbler, Coal Tit, Great Tit, Red-backed Shrike, Magpie, Hooded Crow, Jackdaw, Chaffinch and last but not least Pink Flamingo.

Cattle

Cattle are bred on the island for their meat and milk with the majority of livestock farms situated in the Pyli district.

Dogs and cats

There are large numbers of cats on the island (*most seem to be feral*) and a few dogs wandering free. The majority of the dogs have owners, but they are allowed to wander free during the day. Whether part feral or owned, the dogs are very friendly and pose no problem, except that is for taverna staff who tend to chase them off for the sake of their diners.

Dolphins

Although dolphins are to be found in the whole of the Mediterranean, they are a rare sight in open waters. However, in 2013 pods were seen a number of times from the tourist boats. So keep an eye out, you may just be lucky.

Hummingbird?

You may see during your visit, a tiny flying creature that can easily be mistaken for a Hummingbird. In fact, this will most likely be a Hummingbird Moth, which is native to the island. Sadly Hummingbirds are only found in the New World.

Poultry

Free-range chickens are reared on the island and one thing I can say, having been used to factory-farmed varieties in the UK, is that they taste wonderful, especially when they are cooked on a rotisserie in the Greek way.

Sheep and goats

Whilst sheep and goat rearing is not a prime farming activity on Kos, on your travels you will see large numbers, especially goats, as the resulting meat and milk is an important addition to the islands food production.

Sponges

Look in any gift shop on Kos and it is almost certain you will see sponges for sale as souvenirs and it has to be remembered that these are the remains of a marine animal, not a plant. The nearby island of Kalymnos was once the sponge diving capital of the world.

Wild animals

For those interested in wildlife (*the animal type*), I have added the following information:

Apart from the odd feral goat and cat, wild mammals are scarce and inconspicuous on the island. Especially at night, the occasional brown rat can be seen scurrying across the road, or scavenging near to waste bins. At dusk, bats can be seen swooping through the evening sky feeding on the myriad of insects. The occasional dead hedgehog on the road, especially in the north, bares testament to their presence and in addition, stone martens and brown hares have also been seen on the island.

Greece reportedly supports ninety-five species of land mammals and research shows that Kos shares in this diversity. Research has identified a distribution of twenty-five species of rodent around Greece. However, just four species in total have been reported from the Aegean islands, namely the lesser mole rat, the broad-toothed field mouse, the brown rat and the house mouse.

Getting there

Package holidays

The first and obvious way of visiting Kos is by booking through a tour operator. The major companies that are offering holidays on Kos in 2016 are in alphabetical order:-

Airtours
First Choice (*all inclusive holidays only*)
Jet2.com
Olympic
Thomas Cook
Thomson

A la Carte

Flight only

Most if not all of the major tour companies also offer flight-only alternatives and to give you an idea, the cost of a return flight from the UK into Kos Airport during the summer season, start from around £120 per person. The main holiday companies that also offer flight-only are listed below:-

www.jet2.com

www.thomascookairlines.co.uk

www.thomson.co.uk

UK airlines with direct flights to Kos include British Airways, easyJet, Monarch Airways, and Ryanair. The websites can be found at:-

www.britishairways.com

www.easyJet.com

www.monarch.co.uk

www.ryanair.com

Hotels, studios and apartments

As you can appreciate, there is a vast selection of holiday accommodation on the island, from the luxurious complexes such as the Grecotel Kos Imperial Hotel in Psalidi, all the way down to basic studios. This means that to cover the vast array of hotels and studios on the island to suit all tastes and budgets, I would have to write a book just on accommodation.

My advice would be to first decide on the resort that suits your needs. As they say, one of the most important points is "location, location, location." If you want that quiet relaxing holiday, you don't want to be above a taverna and if you like the nightlife, you don't want to be in the middle of nowhere! Once you have decided on the resort you can search the web by entering, for example, *hotels in Marmari, Kos*. There are a large number of hotel agency websites that offer the full range of accommodation on the island for you to choose from. Once you have your short-list, it is always advisable to check the hotels against review websites such as Tripadvisor.

One point I believe is less important is for your accommodation to offer a restaurant service. One of the joys of Kos is to visit the vast choice of tavernas and restaurants on the island and enjoy what can invariably be attractive surroundings and good food. Who wants to frequent a hotel restaurant, when you can sit by the sea and watch the sun set over the Aegean. If you have a family, you will find that the Greek culture is very family orientated and therefore children are welcomed and catered for by restaurant staff. Most tavernas offer breakfast, either continental or English.

One thing I can confirm is that without exception, the accommodation I have stayed in within Greece in the last 30 years has always been clean and good value for money. You may find that at the budget end of the market, things can be a bit basic as far as room facilities are concerned. However, the top end of the market you can expect a high standard and at a reasonable price.

Most 'self-catering' apartments and studios will have at least a two-ring stove, a fridge and basic cutlery, pots and pans and utensils, a double or two single beds with side cupboards and a wardrobe. Usually there is only a shower with a W.C. For those who like a good night's sleep, it may be advisable if you are visiting in the high season, to select accommodation that has air-conditioning in the rooms. Telephones, televisions and hair-dryers are usually only found in the more expensive accommodation.

Insider tip: *If you are not staying in 'self-catering' accommodation, many hotels and apartments have rules against meals being prepared and eaten in the rooms. I would also advise that where it is acceptable, it is courteous to dispose of any food waste yourself, and not to leave it for the hotel cleaning staff.*

One strange but positive anomaly I have noticed in the past is that room cleaning and laundry changes occur more regularly than is specified in the brochure or room information. You should also find that when the odd problem such as a blocked sink or faulty light arises, raising the issue with the management will invariably result in a quick solution.

An alternative to booking from home is to take a flight to Kos and look for your accommodation when you arrive on the island. You will find there is always some accommodation available and at most times you can negotiate a good price. In Kos Town, as with the other main resorts, there are a number of property companies who may have suitable accommodation on their books, or at least will point you in the right direction.

Camping

For those who enjoy the "back to nature" style holiday, or are looking for a *budget* way of visiting Kos, there is only one campsite on the island. The site is well laid out if a little tired, with shaded areas to set up your tent.

Amenities include hot, clean, showers, toilets and the use of the bar, restaurant and pool in the hotel next door. The campsite is 10 minutes by bus from Kos Town. With prior notice, they also offer the service of picking you up by mini bus at the airport or port.

Kos Camping
Psalidi 853 00 Kos,
Tel. 22420 23275, 22420 23910,
Fax. 22420 23910
Winter Tel. 0210 2432148
Manager: Ms Maria Grigoriadou
Open May - 10th October

Places of interest

Places of interest in Kos Town

On 23rd April 1933, a major earthquake devastated the town and it was the Italians, during their occupation of the island, who laid out the reconstructed street grid plan in a garden suburb format and liberally punctuated the squares with splendid Ottoman and Italianate style buildings. Sadly, since then, modern concrete buildings have sprung up throughout the town, detracting a little from what was once a unique and attractive mix of architectural styles.

Bar Street, which is the street next to the harbour, is the main entertainment area, with a wide selection of bars next to each other. Irritatingly though, you do get hassled by large numbers of touts trying to get you to enter their establishment. However, especially if you are looking for a more relaxed atmosphere, you will find that there are many other bars around Kos Town that serve good cocktails. "Two for one" offers on drinks often means a double measure, not "Buy one get one free"!

Although Kos Town at night is highly commercialised and geared towards the younger visitor, I believe all ages should experience, at least once, the cosmopolitan atmosphere of the island's capital.

Taking all of this into account, Kos Town is still picturesque and interesting. Neatly arranged streets converge on small squares, abundant with flowers, vines and palm trees. The new marina area is worth a visit and there is a wide and inviting promenade behind the harbour for that late leisurely evening walk.

In **Eleftherias Square**, now a pedestrian precinct, you will find the Defterdar Mosque built in the 18th century and some imposing Italianate buildings, one of which houses the **archaeological museum**. In 2014, the museum was extensively renovated.

Eleftherias Square is also the venue for a small enclosed market (*Agora*), selling a wide variety of products including craftware, spices and vegetables.

Castle

One of the main attractions in Kos Town is the **Knight's Castle** (*Neratzia Castle*). The castle was built on the ruins of an earlier fortress and is an imposing sight, situated as it is, at the entrance to the town's harbour. Constructed by the Knights Hospitaller in the 14th century, its completion was constantly delayed by Turkish raids. To further fortify the castle, a second curtain wall was added in the late 15th and early 16th centuries to encircle the first, with a wide and deep sea moat excavated directly below the wall. At the beginning of the 20th century the moat, which connected to the sea, was covered over by Finikon Avenue. The castle, as has always been the case, is entered by a bridge over the moat. In the 15th/16th centuries, alterations were made so that the north end of the bridge could be removed during attack, to further strengthen the already formidable defences.

The castle walls are a patchwork quilt of stone, much of it plundered from the Agora, Asklepion and other ancient sites in the area. As you enter through the impressive 16th century Carmadino gate, you will see a large frieze of the Hellenistic period on the right, re-used as part of the gate. Old basalt columns were also re-employed to strengthen the ceiling of the gate, possibly taken from the early Christian basilica at the port. The gate also displays several medieval coats of arms of the resident 16th century knights. Through the gate you will enter a large precinct containing many statues and pillars.

After crossing the inner stone bridge you enter the second and original bastion, which had four defensive towers. The north-east is completely destroyed, along with a section of the wall in this area. The south-eastern tower is incorporated into the outer wall, all of which have impressive battlements and gun ports.

To your left is the oldest building preserved in the castle, a circular tower bearing the coat of arms of the Grand Masters of the 15th century. The old knights' building at the northern end of the precinct was possibly a warehouse and was restored by the Italians during their occupation of Kos (*1912-1943*).

There is not a great deal to see within the castle, but I would recommend it especially for the views from the battlements. The walls, which are not particularly high on the inside, are worth a climb to take in the panoramic views across the town and harbour.

But one word of warning, especially for those with children, the safety features are minimal and the vertical drop on the outside of the walls is considerable, so extra care should be taken.

The admission charge is 3€.

Hippocrates' tree

The famous **plane tree of Hippocrates** stands in front of the Knights Castle a few metres from the bridge over Finikon Avenue. It is a huge tree, with a circumference of fourteen metres and is considered to be the largest and oldest in Europe. Sadly it is so old it is encircled by scaffolding to prevent it from collapsing!

The tradition is that it was planted by Hippocrates, the "father of modern medicine", who is said to have taught under its shade. However, Hippocrates lived 2,500 years ago and the tree is believed to be less than 600 years old. Tradition also has it that the Apostle Paul taught here, but for the same reason, this is purely a myth. The only possible explanation for the stories is that there may have been a previous tree on the site and this gave rise to the oral tradition.

Hippocrates' tree is a good landmark for starting a tour of the ancient ruins of Kos Town. If you stand with your back to the tree, walk down the slope towards the harbour. At the bottom of the slope is a palm tree, surrounded by a low circular stone wall. Turn left and follow the pedestrian walkway, keeping the orange painted building to your right. Within a hundred metres you will come to the entrance to the site of the ancient Agora on your left. If you continue past this entrance, in a further 200 metres you will enter Eleftherias Square, were you will find the archaeological museum, both of which are covered in more detail in the next section.

Archaeological sites in Kos Town

It was the earthquake of 1933 that allowed the Italians access to many of the ancient ruins in the town that had previously been covered by modern buildings. We therefore owe the Italians a debt of gratitude for seizing the opportunity, especially at a time of great suffering, to both excavate and restore the parts of ancient Kos we see and enjoy today.

I have prepared a guide to the archaeology in Kos Town, including all the main sites and one that takes the shortest route between them. I hope you will find this useful, to help further I have included a map on page 179.

attractions for that rare rainy day, or just to chill from the sun.

Archaeological museum

Situated in the centre of the town, the **Kos Archaeological Museum** is housed in an attractive two-storey building with three arched entrances and contains artefacts from all the historical periods of the island. These are displayed in three rooms surrounding the atrium, which is itself decorated with a beautiful ancient mosaic representing the arrival of Asklepius on Kos. The exhibits also include many impressive statues, reliefs, grave stelae and mosaics from the Hellenistic and Roman periods. A statue of Hippocrates dated to the 4th century B.C. is also on display within the museum.

Closed on Mondays. Entrance fee is 3€.

Ancient town

The original capital of Kos was situated in the southwest tip of the island. It was named Astipalea and flourished in the 6th and 5th centuries B.C.

In the 4th century B.C., after a catastrophic earthquake, the islanders rebuilt the capital in the northwest of the island (*the modern site of Kos Town*). The town was built with an advanced drainage and water supply system and had a fortified port and strong city walls, parts of which have survived to this day.

The archaeological remains are to be found in four main areas of the modern town. These are the port, the western excavations, the east and the central area.

Agora, ancient Greek and Roman city

The construction of the Agora (*Roman Forum*) is dated to the late 4th century B.C. and was one of the largest in the ancient world. The main area of the Agora consisted of arcades on three sides (*north, west and east*) of the central atrium. The northern part of the Agora was linked with the walls of the city, whereas the arcades at the lateral sides probably housed various stores and commercial buildings. The Greek Archaeological Service has measured the total length of this monumental building to be 80 metres wide and over 300 metres long. East of the Agora, excavations have brought to light a portion of the town plan, which followed the Hippodamian system, with broad streets (*4 - 6 metres wide*), consisting of four blocks of houses and commercial premises.

From the back of the Agora walk up the flight of steps onto Hippokratous, turn left and cross the road. A hundred metres on you will come to Mitropoleos on your right. Take this road south until you come to the junction with Korai (*the Cooperative Bank of the Dodecanese is on the corner*), turn right and 400 metres down on your right is what remains of the Temple of Dionysus.

Temple of Dionysus

Situated just after Korai joins the main road Grigoriou E, the Temple of Dionysus is an example of a U-shaped temple of the Hellenistic period. The ruins are dated to the 2nd century B.C., a period of great prosperity on Kos, a fact supported by both the quality and quantity of buildings erected during this period.

The temple was constructed from white and blue-grey marble and consists of two parts, the main altar and the ramp by which devotees entered the temple.

It is believed that the Dionysium was financed by the King of Pergamon, an ally of the city-state of Kos. Sadly the temple was destroyed during the earthquake of 142 B.C. and afterwards was only gradually restored by the local inhabitants. Just the rectangular foundations are well preserved today, along with the south entrance and a vertical stone wall.

By the Byzantine period, the temple had been abandoned and when the Knights Hospitallers conquered the island, they used the site as a quarry in the construction of the castle.

A frieze from the temple, dated to the end of the 2nd century B.C., is now on display in the museum. It presents scenes from the Amazon war and Dionysus with a troupe of maenads and satyrs.

During excavations in the same area, an earlier temple in the Doric style was found, possibly also dedicated to Dionysus, with two rectangular constructions, most likely bases for statues. Italian archaeologists carried out further excavations during the 1930's, but due to World War II, the results were not published.

On the other side of Grigoriou E and slightly further on are the ruins of a large **Roman bathhouse**, dated to between the 3rd and 4th centuries A.D. To the right of the bathhouse is the Casa Romana.

Casa Romana

Highly recommended to visit, Casa Romana was a 3rd century A.D. Roman villa, restored to give a dramatic view of the splendour in which a wealthy Roman citizen lived in this period. The site reopened in 2010 after being closed for seven years and work is continuing to further enhance the visitor experience.

The villa consists of 36 rooms around three atria (*courtyards*) each with central pools. As you walk round you can see how the villa was beautifully decorated with painted frescos and many mosaics, one depicting a panther tearing apart a deer, another dolphins with a sea-nymph on a seahorse.

The largest atrium is bordered by both one and two-storey rows of pillars in an arrangement called a *rodiaki stoa*. The rooms that open onto this atrium contain beautiful mosaics and wall murals. Many other paintings and frescoes are to be found throughout the villa complex.

All the mosaics found in Casa Romana date from 3rd century A.D. A number of statues dating from the late Hellenistic period were also found in the villa, these are now on display in Kos Archaeological Museum.

Opening hours: 08:00-14:00 (*closed on Monday*), entrance is free

Exit the Casa Romana and continue west down Grigoriou E. In approximately 250 metres is the entrance to the Odeum.

Odeum

The Odeum (*or Odeon*) of Kos covers the area west of the restored Casa Romana, this area also housed the Conservatory (*school of music*). According to the inscriptions found on the site, the Odeum was constructed on the site of an older public building.

It has a north-south orientation, with the Koilon (*the semi-circle of seats*) found at the south and the orchestra and scene at the north. Arches, which rest on pillars, support the Koilon; beneath there are two semi-circular galleries containing several small rooms, possibly workshops or storerooms. A number of statues were found in these rooms during excavations, these are now exhibited in the archaeological museum.

The building is dated to the 1st - 2nd centuries A.D, built originally as a venue for music competitions, it also served as the seat of the Gerousia (*Senate*), a local authority with limited power; one important duty being to welcome and honour local dignitaries and influential visitors to Kos.

The Koilon originally had fourteen rows of marble seats; only nine of them have been restored. A passage divided the theatre into an upper and a lower diazoma; four stairways divided the lower part into Cunei. The stage had a pentagonal shape with a proscenium (*the arch over the stage*) and wings. The orchestra pit, decorated with marble, was circular and there were two entrances to the theatre at either side of the stage, both were decorated with fine mosaic floors. Several statues, situated in niches, decorated the entrance arcades of which those found during the Italian excavations of 1929, are exhibited in Kos Archaeological Museum. To the left and towards the back of the Odeum is a small passage which leads to a recently discovered **Roman mosaic**, now protected by a large white canvas roof.

During the summer months, as part of the annual 'Hippocratic Festival', the Odeum places host to a number of music events. Details will be posted on the 'Kos News' page on our website.

Opposite the theatre and at the opposite side of the main road, are the ruins of the western archaeological site.

Western archaeological site

If you are interested in archaeology, the western excavation that includes the remains of Hellenistic and Roman buildings is, I feel, one of the most interesting in Kos Town. However, during my most recent visit, sadly there was a total lack of signs on the site. In late 2013, plans were drawn up by the council to improve the whole archaeological area, including closing the roads to traffic and improving the presentation.

You can enter from Grigoriou E at both ends of the site, the first entrance is just past and on the opposite side of the road to Casa Romana, the second is opposite the Odeum. There is also an entrance at the far north-end of the site, towards the town.

The two main Roman roads that dissect the site are the

Decumanus Maximus, which runs parallel to Grigoriou E and is very well preserved and **Cardo**, nearly opposite the Odeum and running at a right-angle to Decumanus Maximus towards the northern entrance. This was the main Roman road into the city. With its restored colonnades, it gives the visitor a real feel of how splendid the ancient city must have appeared two millennia ago.

House of Europa
If you enter by the Casa Romana gate, walk to the back and directly in front of you are the remains of some fine Roman houses, the best of which is the House of Europa (*Europa was a Greek mythological figure*). The house is named after a beautiful mosaic floor in one room, which depicts Europa being abducted by the god Zeus, who has taken the form of a bull.

From the House of Europa, walk down to Decumanus Maximus and towards the far west of the site. Once there, if you look to your right, the ruins in front of you are of the Nymphaeum.

Nymphaeum
The Nymphaeum was a Roman public bathhouse, ringed by white marble columns and containing some fine mosaic floors. Here you will see an almost intact **calidarium** (*hot room*) with a pool, whilst the **frigidarium** (*cold room*) and pool have been partly absorbed into the adjoining Christian basilica. The Romans built an aqueduct from the hills to the south of Kos to supply the considerable quantities of water required, especially as the Nymphaeum was only one of three major public baths in Kos Town. The Nymphaeum is one of the most elegant examples of a 3rd century Roman public building. To the north of the Nymphaeum are the ruins of the Xisto.

Xisto
The Xisto are the remains of the largest gymnasium on Kos. The name Xisto is derived from fact that athletes scraped (*xisoun*) their bodies in order to remove the oil, which they anointed themselves with, before training and competing. The building contains seventeen restored columns of white marble in the Doric style, out of the original eighty-one that formed the colonnades of the building. The gymnasium was decorated with lion heads, examples

of which can still be seen. In the middle of the gymnasium was a water cistern, where athletes could wash themselves during training. The Nymphaeum was situated adjacent to the Xisto, so that the athletes could bathe and relax after training.

The site is large, so I would recommend a wander round to see all the fascinating remains. You will also see standing prominently above the western archaeological site, the position of the ancient acropolis, now the site of an Islamic mosque with a minaret from which they call the faithful to prayer.

Exit the site at the back north entrance onto Nissiriou and turn left. From here, you are best to refer to a map, but you need to enter Meg. Alexandrou and turn right. Down on your right is the site of the ancient stadium. Once again, on my most recent visit, I found that the site was totally overgrown and therefore I cannot verify whether there are signs to help you appreciate the ruins.

Ancient stadium

The ancient stadium was built at the end of the 4th century B.C. Pillars standing today show a combination of both the Ionic and Doric styles. The length of the building is 180 metres and its width 30 metres. As you look around, note the unusual and partly preserved starting gate.

Exiting the ancient stadium, turn right and right again and a few hundred metres up on your left are the northern baths.

Northern baths and Roman forum

The northern baths are the third of the three Roman public bathhouses in Kos Town. Less dramatic than those in the western archaeological site, but they are still worth a visit. The ruins are on 31st Martiou, referring once again to our map may help. This was also the site of the Roman forum, the focal point of politics, religion and economy in ancient Rome.

This ends the tour of the main archaeological sites in Kos Town.

Green road-train

For those with disabilities, or if you just want a relaxed and brief tour with someone else taking the strain, there is a road-train service (*Greek: Trenaki*) that makes two tours around Kos Town, passing the majority of these sites. Whilst it does give you an overview of Kos Town and the archaeology, it does not stop and therefore you miss the splendour of many of the sites.

The service starts at 10:00, but closes at different times during the season up to 22:00 in high summer. Each tour lasts about 20 minutes and is repeated every 30 minutes. The departure point is at Akti Kountouriotou in the harbour area and costs 5€ for an adult and children go half price. The two routes include the following:

Route A (*10:00 - 14:00*)
   Agora
   Temple of Dionysus
   Casa Romana
   Hippocrates' tree
   Museum
   Western archaeological site
   Ancient stadium
   The harbour area

Route B (*18:00 - 22:00*)
   The evening tour concentrates on introducing the visitor to Kos Town and its many attractions, these include:-

   Kazouli Square
   Eleftherias Square
   K Paleologou Square
   Iroon Politechniou Square
   7th Martiou Square
   Hippocrates' Tree Square
   Konitsis Square
   The harbour area

Green and yellow road-train

This is the Eco-train which heads out of town through the village of Ampavris and on into the countryside and forests of Kos. The tour is aimed at giving you a taste of the beauty and splendor of the island, which lies just a few kilometres away from the busy tourist centres.

You can hop on and off the train if you wish to stay awhile at one of its many destinations, the choice is yours.

The train terminus is near the Municipal building in Kos Town, which is approximately 400 metres past the castle on the main road leading to Psalidi. It departs Tuesday to Sunday inclusive, on the hour from 10:00 - 18:00.

Blue road-train

The blue road-train goes to and from the Asklepion archaeological site, with the same terminus as the Green and Yellow train.

The train runs hourly whenever the Asklepion is open (*usually Tuesday to Sunday inclusive*) and the cost is the same as for the Green road-train. When you arrive at the Asklepion, make a note of the time and a return train should be waiting in an hour's time.

Red (*Elma*) road-train

In 2013, a further road-train route was added to service the Asklepion. The red (*Elma*) road-train runs every day on the hour from 10:00 - 16:00 (*high-season times*). The terminus is opposite the harbour in front of the Kosta Palace Hotel.

Red road-train cost: 5 euro, free for children under 10

After your visit to the Asklepion, there is the nearby village of Platani to visit and refresh yourselves.

Archaeological sites around Kos

Asklepion *(see map page 180)*

Situated 4 km southwest of Kos and near to Platani, the Asklepion is the most significant archaeological site on the island. The excavations began in 1902, undertaken by two archaeologists, Lakovos Zaraftis from Kos and Herr Hertsok from Germany. There are three ways of visiting the site, discounting walking the 4 km from Kos Town. The first is to take the blue and red road-trains that runs between Kos Town and the site, or take a local taxi. The second is to hire a bicycle and the third is by car, if you have hired one. With the latter two, just follow the signs for Platani.

It is still unclear whether Asklepius was a real person or a god, in Homer's "The Iliad", he is referred to as a mortal and in particular "the blameless physician". Whichever was the case, his cult began in the mists of time and he was always associated with medicine and healing, his emblem being a snake coiled around his staff. In the late 6th century, the city of Epidaurus became the prime cult centre and from the beginning of the 4th century B.C., the faith spread throughout Greece. Patients flocked to asklepia, the sanctuaries dedicated to the cult, to obtain help for their illnesses and injuries.

Whilst staying at the sanctuary the patients reported their dreams to the priest-doctors, who prescribed a relevant cure, often a visit to the baths or gymnasium. As snakes were sacred to the Asklepias' cult they were regularly used in the healing rituals. Non-venomous varieties were left to slither on the floors of the dormitories, where the sick and injured lay.

Many famous historical figures both studied and taught at the Asklepion on Kos. The most famous being Hippocrates, but included others such as the famous physician Galen (*129 - 200/216 A.D.*), whose theories dominated western medical science for over a millennium. Later in his career, Galen was appointed as the personal physician to the Roman Emperor Marcus Aurelius (*the Emperor depicted in the film Gladiator*).

The ruins you can visit today are of the sanctuary established in circa 357 B.C., after the death of Hippocrates and which functioned for over a thousand years. The setting is magnificent, elevated on hillside terraces that are connected by a monumental marble staircase. It sits above the village of Platani, with panoramic views across the sea to the Turkish coast.

Little of the original sanctuary remains, due in a large part to repeated earthquakes, Roman alterations and additions and the use of the site as a quarry by consecutive occupiers of the island.

Due to the steep ground, the sanctuary was constructed on three connecting levels, called *andira*. The first is composed of Roman ruins dated to the 3rd century A.D. To your left are the ruins of a large **Roman bathhouse** complex. This andira was surrounded by stoae (*a stoa was a colonnaded walkway, in this case with rooms to the rear for patients*) on all three open sides and at the back, to the left of the stairway to the second level was the medical school. Nothing remains of these buildings, the terrace now being dominated by the arches in the back retaining wall that originally held statues. The patients' spas were also on this level and were supplied with water from an aqueduct running from the springs of King Halkon and Vournika on nearby Mount Dikeo. To the left of the stairs leading to the second level are the remains of a **small temple**, dedicated by Gaius Stertinius Xenophon of Kos, probably to Nero who was known to have been a patron of the Asklepius cult. Xenophon was the personal physician to the emperors Tiberius, Claudius and Nero.

The second level was composed of a large central altar (*4th century B.C.*), the **Temple of Asklepius** of Ionic design (*3rd century B.C.*) and the **Abaton** (*priests' residence*), here the sick waited for the god Asklepius to appear to them in dreams to help cure them.

Behind the Abaton, you can see the remains of a **sacred spring**, with steps leading down to the water level.

Between the second and third levels is a narrow terrace with no obvious building remains and was probably incorporated to strengthen the overall terracing.

The third level was constructed in the 2nd century B.C. and included a large **Temple to Asklepius** of Doric style enclosed on three sides by stoas. Within this stoa complex were also rooms for the patients. Excavations in the surrounding area unearthed a vast array of votive offerings left by pilgrims to the god Asklepius. It is said that the first andira was dedicated to the healing of the body, the second for the soul and the third for the spirit.

The Asklepion was destroyed in the 6th century A.D., it is not known whether by earthquake or invaders. By the time that the Knights Hospitallers arrived on the island in the 14th century, it was a ruin and they used it as a quarry in the building of the castle.

Open Tuesday - Sunday: 8:30 - 15:00. The entrance charge is 4€.

If you enjoy learning about ancient history the **Ancient House-Hippocrates Garden Cultural Centre** is well worth a visit.

The centre is based on life in ancient Greece. The houses are 5th century B.C. replicas, designed to give the visitor a view of how the ancient Greeks lived. All the furniture and decor in the houses has been faithfully reproduced according to ancient designs and on the floors you will see beautiful pebble mosaics. A theatre based on ancient Greek/Roman design is situated in the gardens, where performances and cultural events are regularly held. There is also the **Dimitras Museum** with paintings and artefacts on display.

Off the main island road, take the road to Mastihari and keep going until you see the signs to Black Pearl Beach Bar and Vagi Beach. You should then see the huge red and white electricity building. From there the centre is just a short distance and should be signposted. The centre is also accessible by road from Kardamena and Antimachia.

Entrance fee: 5 euro, 3 euro for children. Tel: 22420 59294

Museums around the island

Folklore museums

Three traditional Kos houses are open to the public in Antimachia, Kefalos and Pyli. The houses are laid out to portray the traditional way of life of the islanders in the past and offer an interesting view of life before the tourist.

Maritime museum

Located in Kardamena and officially opened in July 2002, the museum contains exhibits from the island's maritime tradition and history.

Medical museum

Housed in the international Hippocrates Foundation near the Asklepion, the exhibits include a fascinating selection of ancient medical artefacts as well as sculptures, books, coins, stamps and much more relating to Hippocrates.

Island villages and attractions

Insider tip: *When travelling, don't be put off by the alternative spelling of village names, if it sounds roughly the same, it is likely the same, for example Platani and Platanos.*

The north of the island is rather flat and featureless, with little in the way of scenery except for the views of the neighbouring islands of Kalymnos and Pserimos and the mainland of Turkey. The sea in the north of the island is warmer than the south, but the southern sea is usually much calmer. In the north there is invariably a breeze that can be cooling when the temperature is high, but starting in August, the Meltemi can deliver more uncomfortable winds. Cycling and horse riding are popular in the north due to the flat landscape. The beaches tend to be quieter here than in the south and east.

The south coast is the more developed on the island, due to the endless stretches of sandy beaches. Mountains provide more scenic interest than in the flat north and in the far south, the landscape can get very rugged indeed.

In the following section, I have covered the inland villages and attractions not covered in the *Beaches and resorts* chapter (*in alphabetical order*). If you intend to visit the inland villages, your route will be dependent on whether you are using local transport or hiring, if the latter, what type of vehicle you hire as some roads are only accessible in 4x4's.

Antimachia

Around 5 km inland from Mastihari you will find Antimachia, a picturesque community of whitewashed houses and abundant flowers. Overlooking the main street is one of the most photographed windmills on the island, resplendent with sails unfurled and which, as the last working windmill on the island, is now preserved as a museum.

Antimachia also boasts a **crusader castle** that overlooks the central plain below and the sea beyond. The entrance to the castle is through an imposing gateway and you can climb the battlements from where there are impressive views and great photo opportunities. Two interesting chapels and a folklore museum in the village that are also well worth a visit.

In late August, the village presents their annual **honey festival**, when you can both taste and buy many honey based products. Information will be posted on our website in advance of the event.

South from Antimachia, the island narrows to about 2 km before expanding into the rugged volcanic area of Kefalos.

Asfendiou district

West beyond the Asklepion and at a distance of 14 km from Kos Town is a group of communities, clustered on the slopes of Mount Dikeos and known collectively as the Asfendiou district. Composed of the villages of Asfendiou, Zia, Lagoudi, Agios Dimitrios, Asomatos and Zipári, the district has a combined population of around 3,400.

The picturesque whitewashed houses are set in flower-filled courtyards and there are traditional tavernas and coffee houses. Set in the greenery of the island's thickest forests, this is where you can genuinely be immersed in the traditional Greek approach to life and glimpse what life on Kos must have been like before the package holiday firms arrived.

The village of Asfendiou is one of the most attractive villages on Kos, positioned as it is, overlooking the sea. Numerous stone built houses are dotted throughout the village, with old churches and the ruins of a **Christian Basilica**. In late August each year the village hosts a **wine festival**.

Zia has an **old watermill** that has been turned into a traditional coffee house and the village is the venue for numerous tour buses that stop in the evening to enjoy the dramatic sunsets. The village is known for the friendly inhabitants, who never seem to tire of this tourist onslaught. The tavernas have a reputation for very good food and the village shops sell locally made thyme-honey and olive oil.

A large car park is situated just after the last bend before the village square.

The **Traditional Park of Zia** is situated in the village. With the mountains as a backdrop, the forests stretch out in front of you offering some amazing views. Stone paths, cobbled steps, natural herbs that have been used in traditional medicine for centuries, a vast array of flowers, pine and olive trees and shaded areas with benches all make this a perfect place for you to enjoy a restful walk.

Every now and again you come across domestic and non-domestic animals that have been donated by friends of the park, all of which enrich the experience, especially for children. Towards the top you will find a children's play area which includes swings and slides. A refreshment area is also situated here where you can relax and enjoy a drink or snack.

The park is open until half an hour after sunset.

Entrance is 3 euro for adults and 1.50 for children. Children under the age of 6 go free.

The village of Zipári has the early **Christian basilica of Capama**, dedicated to St. Paul, which has a fine baptistery and mosaics .

Continuing from Zipári, the road passes the ruins of a **Roman aqueduct** before entering the village of Pyli.

Hatziemmanouil winery

On the main road between Kos Town and the airport, just after the exit to Tigaki, you will find the **Hatziemmanouil winery**.

Before 2005 the wine production was located in Kos Town, but was then moved to its present location.

With an area of about 40.000 square metres of vineyards, the winery produces around 20,000 bottles of red, white and rosé wines. Grape varieties include Cabernet, Syrah and Muscat.

The wine is exclusively sold on Kos in some restaurants and supermarkets.

Visitors are welcome to visit and learn about wine making. Entry is free and you can taste and purchase the winery's produce.

Kefalos

The village of Kefalos sits high on a headland with views along the whole southern coast. The old town is an attractive collage of whitewashed houses with brightly coloured doors and windows. Above the village is an **ancient hill fort** from where the views are impressive, but beware, the path leading to it is steep and tiring, especially in the midday sun. Even higher, and forming an impressive backdrop to the village are the twin peaks of Mount Zini and Mount Latia, sadly though, one is spoilt by the addition of radio masts and the other by quarrying.

Kefalos is also where island buses terminate, but there are some lovely walks into the rugged peninsula and if you are really fit, on to Cape Krikelos. Tours are offered locally to a nearby **Byzantine church,** the ruins of **two temples** and the ancient **Astypalia amphitheatre** (*Astypalia was once the island's capital*). The tour also includes a visit to the **Aspri Petra** (*White Stone*) cave, believed to have been inhabited in the Neolithic period.

Insider tip: If you are driving, there are roads that go further into the headland, but beware, especially if you are not in a 4x4 vehicle.

In late September, the village of Kefalos hosts a **fish festival** at the harbour. In the afternoon before the evening event, you can watch the fishermen pulling their nets onto the beach with the catch which will be served to the revellers later. Information on the event will be posted on the 'News' page of our website.

Near to Kefalos, at Pilaiopili, there is an amazing **ruined castle** perched proudly on a pinnacle of rock and affording wonderful views over the hills and sea.

Plaka Forest

One delightful area to visit is Plaka Forest. An ideal spot for picnics and barbeques, the forest is shaded and cool, making it a perfect place to escape from the heat of the mid-summer sun. The air is scented with sweet smelling pine trees and wild flowers that grow in abundance. Streams meander through the area where wild Peacocks and Tortoises roam freely and there is a pond with Terrapins. There are organised picnic areas, tables and bench seats and areas set aside to barbeque food, but remember to take some charcoal!

It's quite easy to find the forest by following the only main road out of Kos Town towards Kefalos. Once you have passed the airport, the road will bend to the left and on the right-hand side you will see a small blue and white church with a sign for Plaka just before it. The road leading to the forest is quite potholed so take care, but keep following it and you come to a small bridge, cross over it and you will arrive at the forest. It is approximately 30 minutes from Kos Town by car. If you want to feed the Peacocks, remember to take some bread!

The best way to get there is by hire car, although some of the Jeep Safaris and other excursions do stop at the forest.

Platanos

Inland from Kos Town is the village of Platanos, the last refuge for the island's dwindling Turkish community. In the 1960's there were around 3,000 Turks living here, but as the enmity between the two countries grew, so the population declined to a few hundred. However, this is still the place for a Turkish night out at one of the many tavernas.

Nearby is a **Jewish cemetery**, surrounded by pine trees. Sadly you will see that the dates on the headstones end abruptly in 1944.

This is when the occupying Germans transported the island's Jewish community to the concentration camps.

Pyli, Armaniou, Agios Georgio and Agios Nikalo

Pyli is the joint name for the three neighbouring communities of Armaniou, Agios Georgio and Agios Nikalo. These are set within verdant countryside, where the main occupation for the villagers is cattle rearing. If you stop at Pyli, there is a **folklore museum** in the village that is worth a visit .

Every year on St. Georges Day, 23 April, the village plays host to horse racing through the village streets, as part of the Saint's day celebrations on the island.

From Pyli a track leads to Palio Pyli, where there are the remains of a **Byzantine fortress** that has within its walls, a church dedicated to the Virgin Mary. A word of warning though, the track to the fortress is steep and rough.

Near to Pyli, at Amaniou, is the ancient **tomb of Charmilou**, a legendary king of Kos and a local hero. The tomb is barrel vaulted with six niches on either side to hold the remains of those buried there. The tradition is that these included Charmilou himself, his family and descendants. The facade of the tomb was originally composed of an Ionic portico made of white marble.

Pieces of the portico appear embedded in the **church of the Cross**, which is built over the tomb of Charmilou, including a marble slab, inscribed with a dedication to Charmilou and the twelve gods of Olympus. The tomb is dated to the late 3rd or early 4th centuries B.C.

Around 2km outside Pyli is a man-made **lake** that was originally built to supply irrigation water to the local farmland. However, in 2013, lighting and a decorative fountain were installed by the Municipality as part of their ongoing plans to develop the area as a tourist attraction.

Visiting Turkey

Bodrum

Visiting Bodrum is easy and highly recommended. If an EU citizen you do not need a visa to enter Turkey for short trips. The easiest way to visit is with one of the local tour companies. I have found these excellent and easy, being picked up and dropped off at your hotel, with an experienced tour guide included. However, for those who prefer to go independently, the ferry cost is approx. 25€ p.p. The currency in Turkey is the Lira (*TRY*) and you will be able to exchange your euro for Lira when you disembark in Bodrum. The exchange rate at the time of publishing this edition was roughly 2.7 Turkish New Lira to the euro.

Bodrum is a beautiful, clean and cosmopolitan city with excellent shopping. Most of the well known international retailers have outlets in the city. You are expected to haggle for every purchase in the local shops, but beware you will be harassed by traders to look inside their shops and then to buy something!

One suggestion you may want to contemplate, especially if you are on a two week vacation on Kos, is to spend more than a day in Bodrum. Pack a few of those basic essentials and make the most of your visit to Turkey. There is not only the nightlife of Bodrum to enjoy, but there are a number of attractions such as the magnificent site of Ephesus to visit, which is 2.5 hours from Bodrum by bus. I would advise that if you do decide to take an extended trip to Bodrum, you discuss the availability of accommodation and potential excursions with one of the many travel agents in Kos Town, or your resort before you depart.

History of Bodrum

The city of Bodrum (*ancient Halicarnassus*) is believed to have been founded in the late second millennium B.C. by Dorian settlers from mainland Greece. However, excavations in the area have revealed artefacts that extend its history back 5,000 years. It is accepted that many civilisations made their home here, for example, the Carians. Homer tells in "The Iliad", that the Carians from Halicarnassus helped to defend Troy against the Greeks.

Under the Dorians, the city became part of the Dorian League. The league included six city-states (*also called the Hexapolis*), with its political centre at the Triopian Apollo temple at Deveboynu, near Cnidus. Meeting there periodically, the members debated issues concerning the economics and politics of the league and held festivals in honour of Apollo. According to Herodotus, Halicarnassus was expelled from the league when a contestant from the city, after winning a sporting event, insisted on keeping the trophy, instead of dedicating it to Apollo.

The city was captured by the Lydians in the first half of the 6th century B.C. and then by the Persians in 546 B.C., after which, it was ruled by the Satrapy of Saird (*a satrap was a governor of a province in ancient Persia*).

In the early 5th century, Halicarnassus was under the control of Artemisia I of Caria. Artemisia was a warrior-woman and leader, who played a significant role in the protection of the Asian Union. She achieved fame as the Admiral of the Carian fleet, allies of the Persians against the Greeks at the naval battle of Salamis in 480 B.C. Although the Persians and their allies were defeated, Artemisia escaped back to the Persian lines, where according to Herodotus, King Xerxes declared "My men have turned into women and my women (*i.e. Artemisia*) into men!" Her son and successor, is notorious for having put to death the famous poet Panyasis and forcing Herodotus (*circa. 484 - 425 B.C.*), the greatest of all Halicarnassians and known as "the father of history", to leave his native city in around 457 B.C.

In 386 B.C., the Persians took complete control of the Carian region (*southwest Anatolia*). This was the start of the most prosperous period for the city, becoming famous for amongst others, a centre of trade and shipbuilding. In 377 B.C., Mausolus, the most famous of the Carian satrapies, became governor of the region. During his rule he ordered the construction of many cities and moved his capital from Milas to Halicarnassus. Mausolus enlarged his new capital by bringing in people from other cities in the region and constructing new city walls, palaces, theatres and temples. However, the most important building in the city was the **Mausoleum**, a monumental tomb constructed for him by Artemisia II, who was both his wife and his sister. It is from this monument that the modern word mausoleum is derived. Construction lasted three years, being completed in 350 B.C. It soon became celebrated as one of the Seven Wonders of the Ancient World.

In 334 B.C., Alexander the Great took Halicarnassus as his army moved through Anatolia on its way to Persia. After Alexander's death the city became the naval base for the Ptolemaic Dynasty of Egypt, which helped to continue its strategic importance in the area. In 192 B.C., the city became a Roman colony and in 88 B.C. was briefly ruled by the Pontus Kingdom, which was centred on the southern shores of the Black Sea.

The first century of Roman rule was chaotic, but the Empire eventually ushered in a period of peace. The prosperity that ensued was unprecedented in Asia Minor and has not been repeated since. Cities grew in number and size, acquiring all the standard amenities of Helleno-Roman civilisation. Stratoniceaia, Kaunus, Iassus, Alabanda, Heracleia and others joined Halicarnassus and Mylasa as major cities. As they grew in number, their individual significance reduced, resulting in the fact that little is known of their individual history during the rule by Rome and then by Byzantium.

In 1071 A.D., Halicarnassus fell to the Seljuk Turks, and it was with the permission of Sultan Celebi Mehmet that the Knights Hospitaller were allowed to construct a castle at Bodrum, the Castle of St. Peter. The castle, with its English, French and German towers, is today the main architectural feature in the town. Sadly though much of the stone used by the knights was taken from the mausoleum, leaving it in the sorry state it is found today.

The city came under Ottoman rule in 1522 A.D., when Suleyman the Magnificent captured Rhodes and forced the Hospitallers to move to Malta. Known as Petrion after the Castle of St. Peter, the city was later renamed Bodrum by the Turks, the name by which it is known today.

Places to visit

Whether visiting Bodrum with an organised tour or independently, I have listed those historical sites that I recommend. Some may not be included in the organised tours, but you should usually be given sufficient time to visit them independently if desired *(see page 181)*.

Amphitheatre

The amphitheatre is another of the prime archaeological sites in Bodrum. Situated on the hillside overlooking Bodrum Harbour, the theatre had a capacity of 13,000 and was built during the Carian reign in the Hellenistic period. The theatre follows the traditional Greek design, which consists of four parts, the edolia (*seating for the audience*), the orchestra pit, the skene (*stage*) and the proskenio (*forestage*). The site became an open-air museum after the excavations in 1973 and during the summer months it features as a venue for concerts. Many ancient rock-cut tombs can also be seen in the cliffs above the amphitheatre.

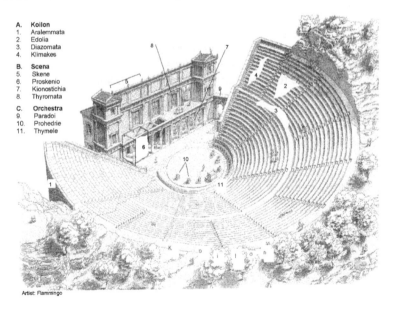

A. Koilon
1. Aralemmata
2. Edolia
3. Diazomata
4. Klimakes

B. Scena
5. Skene
6. Proskenio
7. Kionostichia
8. Thyromata

C. Orchestra
9. Paradoi
10. Prohedrie
11. Thymele

Artist: Flammingo

Bodrum archaeological museum

For those interested in history and archaeology, the museum although small is well worth a visit. It is situated towards the back of the city, so I would advise you ask for directions.

Closed on Monday

Castle of St. Peter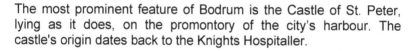

The most prominent feature of Bodrum is the Castle of St. Peter, lying as it does, on the promontory of the city's harbour. The castle's origin dates back to the Knights Hospitaller.

The order was founded in Jerusalem in 1080, to provide care for the poor and sick pilgrims travelling to the Holy Land. After the conquest of Jerusalem in 1099, during the First Crusade, the Hospitallers became a Catholic military order under its own charter and was charged with the care and defence of pilgrims.

Following the loss of Christian territory in the Holy Land, the order operated from Rhodes, over which it had sovereignty and later from Malta, where it administered a vassal state under the Viceroy of Sicily. Although this state came to an end with the ejection of the order from Malta by Napoleon, in essence it survived.

Although the Hospitallers were Catholic, care was denied to no one. When the knights arrived in Bodrum in around 1402, they instructed their builders to remove all usable materials from the tomb of King Mausolus for use in the castle's construction.

The knights referred to the town as Mesy, not knowing that they were in ancient Halicarnassus. The fortress' full name was the Castle of St. Peter the Liberator and served as the prime refuge for Christians from the west coast of Asia during the time of the crusades. The castle remained a stronghold for the knights well into the 16th century.

Under Turkish rule, the castle has undergone several uses including being a military base, a prison and a public bath. But now it is one of the finest museums in this region.

The castle is approached through a series of seven fortress gates and over a moat. Above the gates and incorporated into the castles walls, you can see many finely carved reliefs that were originally part of the Mausoleum.

The castle has five main towers, reflecting the architectural styles and nationalities that made up the ranks of the knights. They are the English Tower, French Tower, Spanish Tower, Italian Tower and German Tower. The fortress walls facing the sea were built thinner than those towards the city, as it was on the latter side, that the greatest protection was required.

Situated within the courtyard is the Gothic Chapel, which houses the **Museum of Underwater Archaeology**, renowned as the world's finest museum dedicated to this subject. Here you will find the amazing Gelidonya Wreck, which was found to have a cargo of copper ingots and dates to 1200 B.C. The wreck was discovered in 1960 during underwater excavations off Cape Gelidonya.

The museum has an extensive range of archaeological exhibits, including amongst many others, Bronze Age objects and weapons from the Mycenaean period, excavated in the necropolis near Bodrum.

To explore the castle completely takes a leisurely two hours and there is an open-air café for a relaxing respite.

Open daily (*except Monday*): 9:00 - 12:00 and 14:00 - 18:00
Admission charge is 10 Turkish Lira (*TRY*), approximately 4€.
Entrance to the underwater museum is an extra 4 Lira.

Mausoleum

The 4th century B.C. Mausoleum of King Mausolus in Bodrum was famous in antiquity, as one of the *Seven Wonders of the Ancient*

World. The marble tomb was as high as a modern fourteen-storey building (*approx. 50 metres*) and from its strategic hillside location, overlooking Halicarnassus and its bay, presented itself as a magnificent sight to all who visited the city.

A reconstruction of the Mausoleum (by Nevit Dilmen)

The Mausoleum was commissioned in 353 B.C. by Queen Artemisia II, in honour of her husband King Mausolus. She spared little expense in hiring some of the best craftsmen and sculptors of her day. The step-pyramid roof was crowned with a large dramatic sculpture of four horses pulling a chariot carrying King Mausolus and his Queen.

A major earthquake destroyed the Mausoleum in antiquity. Then, when the Knights Hospitallers settled on Kos, they used the remains as a quarry in the construction of the castle. Reliefs and other artefacts from the Mausoleum were transported to the British Museum in 1846 and form part of the exhibits to this day.

One of Bodrum's recent literary characters, Cevat Sakir, known as the Halicarnassus Fisherman, asked for the return to Bodrum of the Mausoleum artefacts, presently housed in the British Museum. In a letter addressed to Queen Elizabeth II, he stated that such exquisite works of art were not finding their true place under the foggy and grey sky of London. The reply he received commented: "Thank you for reminding us of this matter, *We* have painted the ceiling of the exhibition room blue."

Sadly little is left of the original Mausoleum to help the visitor appreciate the magnificent splendour of the original tomb.

Open Tuesday - Friday. The admission charge is 10 Lira

Myndos Gate

Located on the west side of the city, the Myndos Gate is one of the two monumental gateways that led into the ancient city of Halicarnassus. The gate formed part of the town's curtain wall and is named after the ancient Myndos Place (*now Gümüslük*), which was the area facing the gate.

It was here in the autumn of 334 B.C., that Alexander the Great, as he moved east on his epic conquests, met considerable opposition during his siege of this Persian controlled city.

Alexander had received a request from Queen Ada of Caria (*which included Halicarnassus*), who had been deposed by the Persians, to help her take back her throne and country. The Persians were mortal enemies of the Macedonians and therefore Alexander agreed and turned his army south towards the city.

Alexander's first attack was against the Milas Gate on the east side of the city (*no remains exist*), but the attempt to take the city through this gate was unsuccessful. After regrouping his forces, Alexander turned his attention to the Myndos Gate on the west, but again met fierce opposition. According to the ancient writer Arrianus, the Myndos Gate was Tripollion in style (*meaning three towers*) and included a moat 8 metres deep and 15 metres wide.

Changing strategy, Alexander had a wooden bridge constructed over the moat and wooden siege towers assembled. The siege towers, full of his finest Macedonian soldiers, were wheeled close to the gate, but the defenders surged out and attacked the towers, siege engines and the Macedonian infantry. The bridge finally collapsed, taking with it the towers and causing considerable panic, with many from both sides drowning in the moat. In the confusion, the gates were shut, leaving large numbers of Persians and their allies on the wrong side of the wall, sealing their fate at the hands of the Macedonians. Although the attack on the gate had been repulsed, Alexander continued to besiege the city.

The Persian generals Memnon and Oronbates, who had been sent by the Persian King Darius III to help defend the city, assessed the situation and realised that with the loss of so many of their soldiers, the outcome was inevitable. Fearing defeat and their certain death at the hands of the Macedonians, they retreated with their main forces to the inner citadel and finally to the harbour, from where they sailed to Kos.

During the latter stages of the siege, Alexander had also realised that his victory was assured. Confident of success, Alexander left 2,500 of his soldiers in the capable hands of his general Ptolomeus (*after Alexander's death, Ptolomeus became Pharaoh of Egypt*) and Queen Ada and left Kos with his main army, to continue his overall campaign in Phrygia.

Soon after Alexander's departure the city fell and in retribution for the inhabitant's opposition and for allying themselves with the hated Persians, Ptolomeus allowed the army to sack the city, during which the vast majority of the city's buildings were destroyed. However, the Mausoleum of King Mausolus, which was respected by Alexander as being one of the Seven Wonders of the Ancient World was spared a similar fate.

The top of the Myndos Gate is now sadly missing, but the ruins on either side show how massive and imposing the gate must have been in Alexander's time, confirming the reason for his initial difficulties in taking the city.

In the last century, tombs made from burned clay, were found and excavated in the vicinity of the gate and were found to date back to Hellenistic and Roman times.

Ottoman shipyard and tower

The recently restored Ottoman shipyard is situated at the northwest of Bodrum Harbour and next to the Marina. The entire Ottoman fleet was destroyed by the Russians in a naval battle at Cesme in 1770. It is believed that the shipyard was established in 1775 in order to rebuild the fleet, utilising the considerable resources of local wood in the surrounding mountains.

Due to an increase in pirate raids, the shipyard was fortified with the addition of the Ottoman Tower in 1794. The tower was restored in 1829 and now serves as a venue for local art exhibitions. During recent restoration of the tower, remains of a Roman bath complex were found in the area.

There is a children's playground and excellent views from here over present day Bodrum.

Modern shipbuilding continues in the many dockyards around the Bodrum area and these are also popular as a tourist attraction. Before you leave Bodrum, it is also well worth a look around the marina, where you will see why Bodrum is becoming known as the St. Tropez of Turkey. You will see, amongst the hundreds of boats, magnificent and luxurious examples of the traditional Turkish Gulet design.

For those who are interested in how the historical events discussed in this book sit within the broader Greek, Roman and European history, I have included timelines on the following pages. Those in bold are mentioned in the book.

Greek timeline

Date	Event
776 B.C.	First Olympic Games
circa 750	**The start of early Greek culture. Homer creates the epic stories "*The Iliad*" and "*The Odyssey*"**
508	Athens becomes a democratic state
490 & 480	**Athenians defeat the Persians at the battles of Marathon (*490 B.C.*) and Salamis (*480 B.C.*)**
circa 450	Athens becomes a powerful state with an empire
472-410	Athens flourishes. Most of the famous Greek plays are written during this period
462-429	Pericles is General of the Greek army and is revered as a great leader
460-370	**Hippocrates, the "father of medicine"**
432	The Parthenon in Athens is completed
431-404	The Peloponnesian Wars between Athens and Sparta
404	Sparta defeats Athens
350	**The Mausoleum is completed, a year after Queen Artemisia's death**
338	King Philip of Macedonia takes control of Greece
336	Kind Philip is murdered, most likely by Alexander and his mother
332	**Alexander liberates Kos from the Persians**
336-323	Alexander conquers most of the known world, as far as India
146	Rome conquers Greece and subjugates it as part of the Roman Empire

Early Roman timeline

Date	Event
509 B.C.	Traditional founding of Roman Republic
396	Romans capture Estruscan city of Veii
390	Rome is sacked by the Gauls after its army is slaughtered at the river Allia
275	The Pharos lighthouse at Alexandria is finished
264-241	First Punic War
218-201	Second Punic War
216	At Cannae, Rome suffers its worst defeat to the Carthaginian Hannibal
202	Hannibal is decisively defeated at Zama
200-196	Second Macedonian war
192-188	War with Antiochus III
171-167	Third Macedonian war
149-146	Third Punic War
146	City of Carthage is destroyed
133	Tiberius Gracchus introduces novel reforms including land grants to the poor and food distribution; he is murdered
123	Gaius Gracchus, brother of Tiberius is also murdered after initiating reforms along the same lines
107	Gaius Marius is elected consul; begins major reforms of army
88	Rome grants citizenship to all free adult males in Italy
82	Sulla becomes dictator

77	Senate chooses Pompey to put down Sertorius's rebellious army in Spain
73	Uprising of slaves led by Spartacus
71	Crassus and Pompey defeat Spartacus
60	Pompey, Crassus and Caesar form the First Triumvirate
59	Caesar elected consul
58-51	Gallic Wars conquest of Gaul by Julius Caesar
53	Crassus dies at the battle of Carrhae
49	Caesar defeats Pompey at Ilerda in Spain. He crosses the Rubicon river; initiating civil war
48	At battle of Pharsalus Caesar defeats Pompey
46	Caesar becomes dictator
44	Brutus, Cassius and other senators assassinate Caesar
43	Octavian, Antony, and Lepidus form Second Triumvirate
42	Antony and Octavian defeat Brutus and Cassius at the battle of Philippi, destroying the last republican army
40	The Roman Senate makes Herod the Great King of Judea
33	Civil war between the armies of Octavian and Antony
31	Octavian crushes the naval forces of Antony and Cleopatra at the Battle of Actium
27 B.C.	Octavian takes the title of Imperator Caesar Augustus; the empire begins

Imperial Rome timeline

Date	Event
27-14 A.D.	Reign of Augustus as Emperor
9 A.D.	Three Roman legions annihilated by Germanic tribes at the Battle of the Teutoburg Forest
14-37	**Reign of Tiberius**
37-41	Reign of Caligula
41	The mad emperor Caligula is stabbed to death
41-54	**Reign of Claudius**
43	Claudius orders the invasion of Britain
54-68	**Reign of Nero**
64	Great fire in Rome. Persecution of Christians
66	Beginning of Jewish revolt
69	The Year of The Four Emperors
69-79	Reign of Vespasian
70	The city of Jerusalem is virtually wiped out by Titus
79-81	Reign of Titus
79	Eruption of Mt. Vesuvius; the twin cities of Pompeii and Herculaneum are buried in ash
80	Colosseum opens
81-96	Reign of Domitian
85	Agricola's campaigns in Britain end.
98-117	Reign of Trajan
101-106	Trajan conquers Dacia. Arabia becomes a province

112-113	Trajan's Forum and Column dedicated
115-117	Jewish revolt
132-135	Bar Cochba's revolt; final diaspora of the Jews. Hadrian's Villa built at Tivoli. Hadrian's Wall built in Britain
142	Wall of Antoninus Pius built north of Hadrian's Wall
162-178	**Marcus Aurelius campaigns in Germanic Wars *(played by Richard Harris in the film Gladiator)***
180-192	The son of Marcus Aurelius, the egotistical Commodus is Emperor. In 192 his chief concubine has him murdered by strangulation
208-211	Severus campaigns in Britain. Arch of Septimius Severus erected
211 - 217	Caracalla is Roman Emperor
284-305	Diocletian's Reign
306-337	Constantine's Reign
312	The Emperor Constantine converts to Christianity. The Edict of Milan grants legal rights to Christians
325	The Council of Nicea - bishops agree the future of the Christian Church
330	Constantine declares Constantinople capital of a Christian Empire
circa 372	The Huns conquer the Ostrogoths
378	Battle of Adrianople, eastern Emperor Valens is killed by the Goths
379-395	Reign of Theodosius
395	Death of Theodosius I, final division into an Eastern and a Western Empire

396-398	The Visigoths ravage Greece
402	Ravenna becomes the capital of the western empire
410	Rome is sacked by the Visigoths
418	Visigoths settle in Aquitaine with capital at Toulouse
429	Vandals cross from Spain to Africa
436	Last Roman troops leave Britain
441	The Huns defeat the Romans at Naissus
circa 450	Beginning of Anglo-Saxon settlements in Britain
451	Aetius defeats Attila at the Catalaunian Plain
453	Council of Chalcedon: Constantinople wins ecclesiastical supremacy over Alexandria
455	Vandals sack Rome
476	Romulus Augustulus - last emperor of the west is forced from his throne by the Germanic chieftain Odoacer, who is proclaimed King of Italy
532-537	Justinian builds the Church of Hagia Sophia
533-534	Re-conquest of North Africa from the Vandals
535-555	Re-conquest of Italy from the Goths
541-543	Great Plague
548	Death of the Empress Theodora
568	Lombards invade Italy
681	The First Bulgarian Empire is formed
690's	Muslims conquer Byzantine North Africa
717-718	Muslims lay siege to Constantinople
1453	Fall of Byzantine Empire when Turks capture Constantinople

Visiting Nisyros

If you have always wanted to stand inside the crater of an active volcano (*when it is dormant of course*) then a visit to Nisyros is a must. The caldera (*crater*) contains active fumaroles (*volcanic vents*), emitting steam, boiling mud and sulphur.

Lying between Kos and Tilos, Nisyros has a surface area of 41 sq. km and a coastline of 28 km. The resident population numbers around 800 (*including just three British expats!*). The majority live in the capital and main port, Mandraki, most of the remaining islanders reside in and around the quaint fishing village of Palli. Palli has a number of good tavernas, hotels and apartments and since 2009 a new marina. Overlooking the town of Mandraki is the Knights Castle that now contains the Monastery of Panagia. If you feel energetic, I recommend you climb the 133 steps that lead up to the monastery and take full advantage of both this famous pilgrimage centre and the magnificent views of the bay and town below.

If not for the volcano, Nisyros should be visited for its "picture postcard" appeal. The volcanic rocks of the island are black and the shops and houses are painted white, with their doors and window frames highlighted in bright colours. Bougainvillea and many other beautiful flowers adorn the village streets and Mandraki has pretty alleyways and a picturesque square shaded by large rubber trees. Near Mandraki is Hohlaki beach with its black pebbles, whereas the opposite islet of Yali has a fine sandy beach.

The volcano

The base of the island is made up of lava flows, with these covered by pyroclastic deposits and volcanic domes. The pyroclastic deposits are related to two explosive volcano events in its history. Each of these events was Plinian in character (*i.e. similar to the great eruption of Mount Vesuvius in 79 A.D.*), producing tall columns of ash as high as 15 - 20 km above the volcano. The collapse of these columns created the pyroclastic deposits. The volume of magma ejected was large enough to eventually cause the summit of the volcano to collapse, creating the 4km by 3km caldera we see today. The two explosive events were probably several thousand years apart and occurred roughly 25,000 years ago. After the caldera formed, further eruptions then produced the lava domes visible today.

A large dual depression, named Rammos and Lakki, is located just east of the centre of the island; it is steep sided with its base being about 100 metres above sea level. Two dacite domes *(dacite is a high iron content rock)*, Saint Elias and Nifios, form the west wall of the caldera. Saint Elias is the tallest peak on the island at 698 metres above sea level. Saint John Mountain is at the eastern end of the caldera.

Stefanos is a small explosion sink, one of five along the southern interior of the caldera. It is about 300 metres in diameter and 25 metres deep. Alexandros, an explosive vent, lies just beyond Stefanos.

It is believed that the volcano erupted in 1422. In 1871, an eruption was accompanied by earthquakes, detonations, and red and yellow flames. Ash and lapilli *(lapilli means little stones)* were ejected and covered the floor of Rammos, destroying the fruit gardens there. During a three-day-long eruption in 1873, a 6 - 7 metre diameter crater formed and ash and blackish mud were ejected.

The area outside of Lakki and Ramos was transformed into a lake by hot saline water that overflowed the crater. The most recent eruption was in 1888, which threw out a cylindrical pipe of volcanic material at least 25 metres in diameter. Mud, lapilli, and steam were also ejected. In 1956, fumaroles were observed along the west and south sides of Rammos.

The local tour agents charge much less than the holiday tour operators, so my advice is to shop around. The trip to the crater is by bus and is safe, but the road does zigzag down the crater wall with some steep drops that can be a bit unnerving for those with vertigo. I would also advise that you don't wear flip-flops, as they could melt as you walk on the hot surfaces within Stephanos!

Organised trips

Most tour companies will offer a selection of excursions to their customers at the traditional "Welcome Meeting". These range from the sometimes-abused title of a "Greek Night", day boat trips around the island including a barbeque, to more exotic options such as a trip to Bodrum, Turkey.

Many of the excursions can also be found independently, through the many tour companies situated in the towns on the island. Whilst the choice is down to the individual, before booking with your tour operator, I would recommend you shop around to see what offers are available and if possible talk to other holidaymakers who have already been on the tour in question.

The cost, especially for a family can be considerable. For example, a one-day tour of Bodrum with one of the major holiday companies for a family of 4, with two children under 12, will cost around 200€ and this does not include food and drinks.

To give you a flavour of what is available from the independent tour operators on the island, I have outlined a selection offered by Tigaki Tours, whose offices are in Tigaki and Marmari. I have personal experience of this company's tours and have found them excellent, tel: 2242069494.

Nisyros (*excluding 2€ local tax per person*)	28€
Three island cruise (*Kalymnos, Plati and Pserimos*)	28€
Visiting Turkey (*Bodrum*)	28€
Coach tour of Kos	28€
Visiting Rhodes by hydrofoil	38€
Thermal springs	8€
Fishing day including BBQ	28€

Tony Oswin

Beaches and resorts

The beaches and resorts

Symbols
- ⓘ Restaurant facilities
- 🍸 Bars
- 🏄 Water-sports
- 🆁 Blue flag beach (*International quality beach award*)
- 🤿 Scuba diving

Beach facilities can change without warning, the following are correct at the time of going to press.

Kos Town beaches 🤿

Kos Town doesn't actually have a beach just a harbour, but Lambi beach is north of the harbour and Psalidi beach to the south.

The view from these beaches, across the sea to Turkey, is an added attraction and the sea is clear and good for swimming and snorkelling. The proximity to Kos Town is a plus for those who like holidays with a good nightlife and who do not want to commute.

Lambi ⓘ 🍸 🏄 🆁

Lambi beach on the north side of Kos Town harbour is the better beach, being much larger than Psalidi and having more tavernas and sunbeds. However, once again the beach consists largely of pebbles and shingle and can get very busy, being next to the main town.

The western end of Lambi beach, near the army-training base and towards Tigaki, is usually less crowded and is sandier. Like all northern beaches, it can get windy and the sea can be rough. The beach is long and shelves gently enough to make it safe for children when the sea is calm.

Part of Lambi used to be occupied by the military, but the Greek army has long since lost the battle with the tour operators, who are packaging up the place with almost military precision.

Psalidi ⓘ ⓣ ⓢ ⓢ

Psalidi beach is the less appealing of the two near Kos Town, it is small and consists mainly of pebbles and shingle and tends to be full of sunbeds. Nearer town the beach is narrow and can be noisy and access to the beach is down steep pathways. There are a limited number of bars/tavernas lining the beach and two supermarkets in the area. A broad selection of water-sports is available including banana boats, jet skis and sub-aqua. Blue Beach in Psalidi has a pleasant grassy area on which to sunbathe. If you are staying at one of the hotel complexes in Psalidi, such as the Kos Imperial, the hotel beaches are well maintained and of a higher quality.

Travelling southeast, Psalidi marks the start of a long trail of beaches leading all the way to the cape of Agios Fokas and on to the resort of the same name.

Main beaches around the island, clockwise from Psalidi:-

Therma (*Embros Thermi*)

Therma beach lies just south of Agios Fokas and in easy reach by bus from Kos Town (*a 15 minute journey*). Ask for the bus that terminates at the beach and there will be no worries about where to get off.

The beach is narrow and protected from the worst of the winds by high cliffs. The sand is black, consisting primarily of volcanic grains. One problem that affects the beach is a strong smell of sulphur that emanates from the hot springs. The sea here is ideal for swimming and snorkelling and due to the hot springs that empty into the sea. One experience you can encounter is the strange sensation of alternate hot and cold waves breaking over you. Many people visit the Therma area specifically to obtain the curative powers that are said to be associated with these hot springs.

To get to the main springs by car can be a bit tricky as the road seems to go on forever and the track is steep, rocky and potholed. If you are visiting the springs or beach by car, it is advisable not to leave anything in your vehicle. I would also suggest you leave the glove box open to show there is nothing worth stealing. Sadly in recent years there have been instances of vehicles being broken into and valuables stolen.

Insider tip: *If you are walking, you need to accept that it is a long steep trek back up to the road after your visit.*

Kardamena ① 🚊 🖻 🖼

Kardamena has sadly suffered more than most from the tourist trade. A generation ago the village was picturesque and known as a centre for fishing and fine ceramics. Too many bars, discos and burger outlets have diminished its Greek charm, but for those younger visitors, it may offer the *high octane* amenities they are looking for. I can certainly say though, that if you are looking for a traditional Greek village atmosphere, with charming streets and a good choice of quality tavernas, Kardamena is not for you.

New hotels, bars and cafes spread out on both sides of the resort for 5 km. Although the whole area offers wide sandy beaches, they can get very crowded in the high season. At the northern end of Kardamena are the self-contained package holiday resorts of Norida and Summer Palace.

On the beaches at Kardamena you will find a wide variety of water-sports and amenities. This means, that those closer to the water sports and amenities can get very busy and their cleanliness can therefore suffer.

Beware when bathing from the beaches, as in many places there are very sharp submerged rocks, making it easy if you are bare-foot to receive nasty cuts to the feet. However, if you walk down past the Emiliana towards the Posidonia taverna the beach has more sand, making it much easier and safer to walk into and swim.

Insider tip: *There is a small clean sandy beach near to the Banana Bar, which tends not to suffer from the excesses of the main resort.*

At Kardamena there are the ruins of a Hellenistic theatre and early Byzantine basilica.

From Kardamena you can catch a boat to the volcanic island of Nisyros, a visit I highly recommend and have featured in this book.

Between Kardamena and Agios Stefanos is a long stretch of sand parcelled up into beaches with anglicised names. These in order are Tropical, Magic, Sunny, Banana, Paradise and Camel. I will cover these in this order.

Tropical

Tropical beach is a naturist beach and is located approx 2.5 km south of Kardamena, heading towards Kefalos on the coastal road. The beach is set lower down from the road and is 0.5 km past a large block of apartments. Parking is available just behind the beach and a local bus service from Kos Town stops here.

The beach is sandy, but the water line for half of the beach consists of flat rocks, making access to the sea a little tricky. The beach therefore doesn't tend to get too busy in the high season.

Banana

Banana beach (*also called Lagada beach*) is very clean and one of the most picturesque in this area, with Juniper bushes straddling the low sand dunes behind the beach.

Magic

Magic beach (*also called Poleni beach*), is the longest, broadest and most natural of all these beaches. Although it is one of the quietest, there's no shortage of sunbeds. To date there are no water-sports and the only refreshments available are from a taverna just above the beach. The northern end of the beach, past the hand-made stop sign, is reserved for naturists.

Access to the beach is via a track that has been carved out of the hill. It is metalled, but there are potholes and sheer drops with no barriers, so my advice is to be careful.

Sunny ⓘ ⬀

Sunny beach is a 2 km stretch of clean white sand. With few hotels and being less well known than some, the beach usually has plenty of empty sunbeds. However, it does suffer from a lack of bars and tavernas, so my advice is take your own supplies. Composed mostly of sand, the beach shelves gently into the sea and has no exposed rocks or sudden dips. The sea is usually calm and is therefore good for swimming and snorkelling.

Paradise ⓘ ⛕ ⬀

Paradise beach is also known as Bubble beach, on account of the underwater volcanic vents that are a feature of a number of beaches on Kos. To see these vents, you need to wade or swim out a short distance and preferably use a snorkel, but beware of getting too close, as the emerging water can be extremely hot.

The beach does live up to its name, being a long sandy sheltered beach with a shallow sea, making it ideal for children. A word of warning though, keep an eye on the very young, as they can easily get lost among the rows of sunbeds.

Being very popular, it can get overcrowded and because of this, has become over commercialised. The water is shallow enough for both children and none swimmers to enjoy safely and there is a small water park for the more energetic. The beach also offers a wide variety of water-sports and amenities for the more adventurous.

You can take the speedboat from Kefalos to Paradise beach for 5€

per person (*the last return journey is at 17:30*). Sunbeds are 7€ for the day and food and drink is available on or near the beach and is reasonably priced.

It should be noted that Magic, Sunny and Paradise are in effect one long stretch of beach, between Kardamena and Kefalos.

Camel (*Kamila*) 🕮

Camel beach is very pretty and is composed of fine to coarse black and gold sand, with interesting rock formations under the clear water making it ideal for snorkelling. It is less popular than others due to the steep access road that leads down to the beach. It is a favourite with nudists, mostly Swedish and Dutch.

Agios Stefanos 🕮

Two kilometres north of Kamari is Agios Stefanos. This is a small beach consisting of pebbles and shingle, with the best section being near the Club Med; the facilities here are open to the public. The Club Med is next to the ruins of St. Stefanos and near the St. Stefanos islet, which has a small fisherman's chapel. I have to say though that the Club Med has, in my opinion, spoilt what was a very pretty area.

This beach has clear blue water and you only have to wade out a few metres to be surrounded by small fish swimming around you. The sea here is good for snorkelling and a wide range of water-sports facilities is on offer. There is a road down to the beach that ends in a small car park next to the taverna.

At this point the island is only 2 km or so wide and even south facing beaches like Agios Stefanos, have little protection from the strong Meltemi winds when they blow.

On the nearby headland are the remains of two well-preserved triple-aisled 6th century Christian basilicas. The ruins contain beautiful bird mosaics. Sadly they are usually covered to protect them from the elements.

Kamari/Kefalos ⬤ ⬤ ⬤ ⬤

The beach from Agios Stefanos stretches south to Kamari and its location and amenities are very good, but sadly it suffers from having a pebble and shingle beach, so it is advisable to wear flip flops in and out of the sea. Kamari beach is the beach area for the village of Kefalos and can be named in either way in holiday brochures.

The best sand is located close to Agios Stefanos, where the beach is completely monopolised by the Club Med resort. The sea is beautifully clear and clean. There are plenty of sunbeds available, not too close together and they are usually cushioned with a fitted pillow. The beach gradient is steepish, which is a plus as you can swim rather than walk on the pebbles; however there are still shallow areas where children can play.

A number of tavernas and bars directly service the beach. The water-sports centre in the bay is very popular and the staff are friendly and helpful. The sports available include hiring a pedalo (*around 15€ for an hour*), jet skiing (*35€ for 15 minutes*) to water skiing, banana boats, ringos (*large inflatable rings, pulled behind a speedboat*), parascending, wakeboarding and windsurfing.

Behind the beach, there is a comprehensive shopping area that caters for most tourist needs. There are a range of tavernas and bars offering a broad selection of food and drink to suit most tastes.

On or around September 19, the harbour at Kefalos will be the venue for the annual fish festival. Please check our website nearer to the date for confirmation of times and date.

Wave ⬤ ⬤

One further beach in the area, which is a well-kept secret, is Wave beach. You need transport, but it is well worth it. It is not a sandy beach, but there are sunbeds and some romantic coves. So if you are looking for privacy and a lovely setting to sunbath, ask a local in

Kefalos and they should be able to direct you.

Mastihari ① ⛱ 🏊

Mastihari is an attractive beach composed of fine white sand with the beach shelving gently into the sea, receiving refreshing breezes on most days.

As it is known as one of the best beaches on the island, it does suffer a little from its own success and can get very crowded. Many of the package holiday companies have chosen Mastihari as one of their main destinations which adds to the problem, especially near the village.

If you want to have a hundred metres or so of beach to yourself, there are areas of the beach away from the village (*the beach is 2km long*) where you can find a bit of peace and tranquillity. Troulos Beach, halfway between Mastihari and Marmari, is the only 'Blue Flag' beach in the area.

Behind the beach there is a good selection of tavernas and behind these the village offers a selection of mini-markets, shops, cafes and small bars in an attractive and traditional setting of narrow colourful alleyways.

At the western end of the beach are the remains of a 5th century Christian basilica.

The long harbour wall stretches out to sea for 200 metres or so and it is here that you can catch one of the frequent ferries that leave for the nearby islands of Pserimos and Kalymnos.

Marmari ① ⛱ 🏊

Marmari is a very clean, sandy beach with low-lying dunes behind. However, there has and continues to be a considerable amount of new development, especially with regard to self contained hotel complexes and therefore one of the downsides of this is that the area is poorly served by facilities such as tavernas, bars and shops. Like most of the northern beaches it can get very windy, but is slightly more sheltered from strong winds than other nearby beaches. Marmari enjoys quieter seas than Tigaki and the beach shelves gently into the sea, though the waves can get large.

The main resort is very popular with Germans, with UK hotels being rather isolated along this shoreline. There is a go-karting circuit just behind the beach.

Tigaki ⓪ ⓣ ⓢ

The sea at Tigaki is shallow and shelves gradually, but when the wind is strong, the currents can make the beach less suitable for small children and lilo's, but ideal for windsurfers. As with most beaches, the further away from the town centre you go, the more peaceful the beach becomes.

The beach is clean and is composed of good white sand backed by low dunes. The quality of the sand improves the further you go towards the area called Alikes, which is composed of saltpans and marshes. Beware of settling too near the sea, as passing cruise liners can send waves crashing onto the shore and only those near the dunes will survive the wash!

Turkey and Pserimos are your views out to sea and the mountains of Kos form the backdrop.

The facilities in the area are very good, with many shops, bars and tavernas. A wide range of water-sports is also available, such as jet-skis, banana boats, ringos and windsurfing. These can be found approx. 100 metres north of the resort square.

There is a naturist beach at Tigaki at the northern end, near the salt lake.

Activities for the very young

If you have booked hotel accommodation through a tour company, most offer activities for the very young within the hotel precincts and these should be listed in the company's brochure, or via the representative. However, other than the obvious days on the beach, I will outline a choice of activities that are suitable for children.

In or near most of the main resorts, you can usually find a limited number of fairground attractions for an evening treat, including dodgem rides, toy train rides and mini-carousels.

Boat trips around the island can be booked in most resorts, as can pedalo hire, banana rides and paragliding. The horse riding stables on the island also offer pony rides for the young. Both of these are described in more detail later in the chapter on *Sports and recreation*.

Most of the larger supermarkets and souvenir shops stock a wide range of toys, including such things as childrens' fishing kits, snorkelling sets and fun beach items, such as bucket and spades, lilos, toy dinghies, frisbees, beach balls, racket ball sets, etc.

All the usual UK battery sizes are available in the supermarkets, but make sure the kids bring the battery chargers for their games consoles and equipment, or suffer the consequences!

The internet cafés on the island tend to attract the younger user and it may be an idea for them to bring any favourite computer game software with them, although most have games already loaded.

Water park

There is now only one water park on Kos, namely Lido Water Park near Mastihari. This is a good venue for children, having a multitude of attractions, such as slides, water flumes and wave machines. Entrance fees are around 20€ for an adult and 15€ for children under 12. The entrance fee is for the whole day, so be prepared!

On site there are snack bars, bars and restaurants, but remember these extras can add quite a lot to the cost of the day. The opening hours are from 10:00 until 19:00.

Pubs, clubs and adrenalin

Being the second most popular tourist island of the Dodecanese after Rhodes, Kos has a vast selection of nightlife. Most of the lively bars and nightclubs of Kos are concentrated around Bar Street in Kos Town and in Kardamena. For example there are eleven clubs in Kardamena alone, but true to my word of being unbiased and independent, I have not added a definitive list.

The bars and clubs also cater for different tastes and therefore one seen as cool by one person could be totally un-cool to others. My suggestion is to talk to the locals and those who have already sampled what's on and make your own decision.

Pubs

Kos Town and the other main resorts are bursting with bars and pubs and there's something to suit everyone *(in Kardamena alone there are around sixty bars and pubs)*. From the latest dance anthems to the cheesiest tunes, a great indie scene and a splash of funky house and R 'n' B, the music is non-stop and the bars can get packed with revellers. Music is usually played until midnight, when if you still have the energy, the clubs take over.

Clubs

As good as the bar-life is, if you want to go clubbing, holidays on Kos will still live up to all your expectations. Bars are free to enter, but most clubs charge around 3 - 8€ entrance fee. Prices for drinks at the venues around the towns are quite reasonable, probably the same if not a little cheaper than back in the UK.

The club opening hours are:-

Sunday to Thursday: 12 midnight - 4 am
Friday and Saturday: 12 midnight - 6 am

Adrenalin

There's so much to do and yet days can be as chilled out or action-filled as you like. For adrenalin junkies, don't miss the speedboat trips and loads of other exhilarating water and land-based activities. For the more laid back, relax and catch some rays, or check out the island, Nisyros, or even take that trip to Turkey.

Or how about a Jeep safari, you will find these advertised in the local tour company offices. Dependent on the company, they either pick you up at your hotel, or from a convenient collection point. You will travel in a convoy of jeeps following an experienced guide over mountains, through forests and down dirt tracks to the coast. This is a great day out, taking in the lovely landscape of Kos and its villages. Lunch is organised along the route at either a taverna, or alternatively, a picnic or BBQ on the beach.

One word of warning though, take plenty of sun-tan lotion and some good protective clothing, as with jeeps being open to the sun, you can come back looking like a lobster and don't forget the driving licence!

Another great day out is a visit to Kalymnos, the nearest large island and once renowned as the sponge capital of the western world. The island retains much more of the traditional Greek culture and architecture than Kos. Ferries/hydrofoils or organised tours can be booked at the travel agents in the main Kos towns and resorts.

Getting around

For those who want the convenience, hiring a car is easy on Kos and the driving conditions are good. If you are on the island for more than one week, it may be worth hiring a car for only some of your stay as the local bus service is pretty reliable, air-conditioned and regular. I have included bus information in a later chapter.

Obviously this mode of transport is dependent on where you are staying and how accessible your hotel/apartment is to the local bus services. Most of the supermarkets on the bus routes sell tickets and will confirm the bus times.

Taxis are plentiful and in Kos Town can be found in the harbour area, near the Dolphin roundabout and outside the Alpha bank. The main taxi station has now been moved out of the main town centre. Kos taxi-drivers are expected to speak English but the rule sometimes doesn't seem to be followed stringently. Taxi fares are fixed and to give you an idea of the cost, the price per kilometre is 1.20€, therefore from say Kos Town to Tigaki will cost around 16€. **The latest taxi charges can be found on our website**, on the 'Kos Travel Info' page.

Insider tip: Although the taxi companies are very honest, to prevent any misunderstanding, it is always best to confirm the price of the journey before setting off.

Taxi telephone numbers: 22420 22777 and 22420 23333

If you decide to hire a car and you are travelling with a tour company, I am sure they will offer to arrange a hire car for you. Alternatively there is a broad range of small car hire companies on the island and my experience is that they are all of high quality and open to *a* little negotiation, especially at the beginning and end of the season. You can budget on paying around 240€ for one week's hire of, for example, a Daewoo Matiz or equivalent, which includes air conditioning (*a must especially in the high season*) and power steering, with prices increasing to around 340€ for the top end specification of a jeep. However, take account of the fact that although a jeep is seen as more of a fun vehicle and will go where the lower slung 2WD cars won't, it is open to the sun which is nice at first, but you can return home looking like a beetroot! There is also nowhere to securely lock-up your valuables.

I am not being condescending, but remember to bring your driving licence with you, an obvious thing you may say, but you would be surprised how often people forget and can't hire a car. For non EU residents, you are required by law to have an *International Driving License*. Also beware, if you park illegally the police will remove your registration plate and you will have to go and collect it from the police station, as well as of course, pay the appropriate fine.

Seat belts are compulsory and children under 10 are not allowed to travel in the front of the car. "Drinking and Driving" is a serious offence with harsh penalties, whether you are on two wheels or four. Police roadblocks for breath-tests, are a regular occurrence all year round, especially in the summer months.

When travelling around the island, please be careful when parking in the villages, the roads are very narrow and the local buses weave their way through, with usually inches to spare between the bus and the houses. You will therefore be in trouble if you block the road.

I would also recommend that you take note of the advice of the car company as to which roads your particular vehicle is appropriate for. Many of the un-metalled interior roads look fine as you enter them, but they usually get progressively worse, with large potholes and sometimes with nowhere to turn around. If you don't hire a 4x4 take care, or you may find yourself facing a hefty bill for any resulting damage to the car.

Fuel is readily available with modern service stations throughout the island. Prices per litre are on average around 1.70€ and that includes the personal service of an attendant filling the tank.

Roads are reasonably good between the resorts, but the one thing that will amaze the visitor, is the lack of traffic on many of the minor roads, with the main road from Kos Town to the airport and Kefalos being the only one you could reasonably call busy.

Scooter, motorbike, scooter, quad bike and buggy hire

Now we come to the hire of the two-wheel mode of transport. Although initially very attractive, especially to the younger visitor, as the cost is low and there are many hire companies promoting them, I have seen so many serious accidents involving motorbikes or scooters in Greece, that I would recommend anyone young or old, to think again and if they can afford it, indulge themselves in the extra cost of a car.

Although all the hire companies supply crash helmets, most people you see on two wheels, are dressed in shorts and T-shirts and I have seen the result of flesh contacting tarmac and gravel. Even at low speeds, the resulting injuries are enough to put anyone off the idea for life!

If it's a more exciting mode of transport than a car that you desire and price is not a crucial consideration, then most motorbike rental shops offer 4 wheel quad bikes for hire. The daily hire charge is around 50€. Please note though, that most travel insurance companies now class quad bikes as a "dangerous sport" and do not cover their use. One unfortunate UK tourist to the island in 2012 was injured on a quad and had to be repatriated. His insurers (*a quality company*) dismissed his claim and he was left with a bill for £15,000!

However, I believe a safer alternative to a quad is the 'new kid on the block', a buggy. Compared to quads they are much safer as their centre of gravity is lower and most models have a roll bar and safety belts as well as other extra features. Many hire companies are now offering this alternative to the quad and at a similar, if not the same, hire price.

With regard to pedal cycles, I have noticed a surprising number of visitors using this form of transport, although there are a lot of hills on Kos. For those who do enjoy cycling, I have included information on cycle hire in the chapter on *Sports and recreation*.

Finally, be careful whichever mode of transport you decide on, as the Highway Code is not stringently followed, especially at cross roads and with regard to "the right of way".

For the more adventurous, there are daily ferry and hydrofoil services to the other Dodecanese islands as well as the Turkish mainland. I have outlined the information in the chapter on *Ferries and hydrofoils*, but more detailed information can be obtained from the port in Kos Town, or the local travel agents.

Bus information

Bus information

The Kos Town buses (*DEAS*) run routes around the town while KTEL buses take you everywhere else. Buses are frequent to the main resorts. The main bus station is in Kos Town, on Kleopatras Street. Tickets are bought on the bus although you get up to 30% off if you buy at the bus station.

The latest schedules are posted at Kos Town harbour and at the bus station. Timetables are available free of charge, both in Greek and in English. Most DEAS town buses operate from the bus stop on the south side of the harbour.

There are three tourist road-trains operated by KTEL. The green train offers two alternative trips around Kos Town, the green and yellow train takes you on a tour out into the beautiful Kos countryside, and the blue one ferries visitors to and from the Asklepion (*see page 50*). The ride is very bumpy, but it is the only public transport to the Asklepion from Kos Town. The cost is 5€, children go half price.

Food and drink are not allowed to be consumed on-board the buses and you should wear a top when travelling. This is to prevent sweat and suntan oil soiling the seats.

When I wrote my first book on the island of Thassos, I initially included all the bus times, but one quirk of Greek transportation is that timetables can change without notification. I have therefore included on the next page a KTEL bus timetable from 2015, purely as a guide to routes, price and frequency. As the timetables can change without notice, I cannot guarantee all will be correct. **The latest bus timetables can be found on our website** on the 'Kos Travel Info' page. You will also be able to obtain the latest timetable locally, but if your journey is time sensitive, please double check.

Inter-city bus (*KTEL*) tel.: 22420 22292
Inner-city bus (*DEAS*) tel.: 22420 26276

Kos Bus Timetable

(If your journey is time-sensitive, please check the bus times locally as they can change without warning.)

Departures from Kos	Monday to Saturday	Sunday	One Way Ticket	Departures from villages	Monday to Saturday	Sunday
Kos to Asfendiou and Zia	07:00 08:40 13:00	-	2 €	Asfendiou to Zia and Kos	07:30 09:00 13:30 15:30	-
Kos to Tigaki	03:00 10:00 13:00 15:00 16:00 18:00 21:00	09:00 10:00 13:00 16:00 18:00	2€	Tigaki to Kos	09:25 10:25 13:25 15:25 16:25 18:25 21:25	09:25 10:25 13:25 16:25 18:25
Kos to Marmari	00:00 10:00 13:00 15:00 16:00 18:00 21:00	09:00 10:00 13:00 16:00 18:00	2€	Marmari to Kos	09:25 10:25 13:25 15:25 16:25 18:25 21:25	09:25 10:25 13:25 16:25 18:25
Kos to Pili	07:00 10:00 13:00 15:00	07:00 13:00	2 €	Pili to Kos	07:30 10:20 13:20 15:20	07:30 13:20
Kos to Mastichari	09:00 10:20 13:00 14:30 16:30 21:00	09:00 13:00 17:00	2.90€	Mastichari to Kos	08:00 09:40 10:40 11:25 15:40 17:30	08:00 09:40 16:15
Kos to Antimachia	13:00 21:00	13:00 17:00	2.40€	Antimachia to Kos	07:50 17:25	07:50 16:10
Kos to Airport and Kardamena	05:00 10:20 13:00 14:30 16:30 21:00	09:00 13:00 17:00	3.20€	Kardamena to Airport and Kos	07:50 09:50 11:10 15:30 17:15	07:50 09:50 16:00
Kos to Airport, Paradise Beach and Kefalos	09:00 13:00 14:30 21:00	09:00 13:00 17:00	4.40€	Kefalos to Paradise Beach and Kos	07:30 10:00 15:00	07:30 10:00 15:45

Ferry and hydrofoil information

Kos to Bodrum

You can step into Asia for the day by taking the ferry to the bustling town of Bodrum, just across the straights from Kos. Haggle for carpets, leather goods, jewellery and *genuine* fake Rolex watches! Alternatively you can explore the ancient sites in this historic town, such as the Mausoleum, the ancient theatre, the Crusader castle and the Myndos Gate besieged by Alexander the Great.

There are daily excursion boats to Bodrum leaving at 8:30 each morning and returning at 16:00 in the afternoon. You can obtain information and book tickets at one of the local travel agencies in the main towns, or at the port in Kos Town.

The main Turkish hydrofoil company, Bodrum Express, run a daily service in the summer months that leaves Kos for Bodrum at 16:30 in the afternoon. The Bodrum to Kos ferry is at 09:30 in the morning.

The ferry companies can offer a useful pick-up service when you book in advance. A minibus collects you from your accommodation or a central pick-up point and takes you to the ferry port (*usually at no extra charge*).

Insider tip: *A word of warning, the queue at both the Kos and Turkish passport controls can be long and slow in the height of summer. So make sure you are at the ferry port early, as it can be nerve-racking realising your departure is in 5 minutes and you are still well down a very slow moving queue.*

Kos Port Authority telephone numbers: 22420 26594
: 22420 26595

Kos to the other islands of the Aegean

Daily ferry connections are available from Kos to Rhodes and Piraeus.

The island is also linked with the rest of the islands of the Dodecanese and with Mykonos, Syros, Samos and Thessaloniki.

Daily hydrofoils also serve the islands of Samos, Ikaria and Fourni in the north-eastern Aegean and in the summer months you can take the hydrofoil to Rhodes and Samos.

Excursion boats

Boats leaving from the harbour of Kos Town operate excursions to Bodrum and the islands of Kalymnos, Pserimos, Plati, Nisyros and Giali. From the port of Kardamena, excursion boats go to Nisyros and from the port of Mastihari, to Pserimos and Kalymnos.

There are also excursion boats that go from the main resorts to various beaches on the island and return later in the day.

If you are interested in boat trips, I would advise that you get details of what's available at a number of tour operators and compare details and prices.

Eating and drinking

In this chapter I will first cover dining out. During the writing of this book I have meticulously sought to be unbiased and accurate with all the information I have included. However, where dining out is concerned, we have all had the disappointing experience of a poor meal in a highly recommended restaurant. Both differing tastes and changing circumstances can mean that a good restaurant to one person can be unacceptable to another. Also, as most restaurants on the island are seasonal, staff tend to move from one establishment to another, year to year and even during the season, which can affect the quality. Therefore in this chapter, I believe it is wise not to recommend any particular restaurants or tavernas on the island, but instead try to outline some basic information and useful hints.

The tips I would pass on are as follows:

First take a good look at the taverna or restaurant in question, is it busy, does it have pleasant surroundings? A major part of dining out on holiday is, I believe, the service, surroundings and views. Are the locals eating there, as they are more knowledgeable of the best eating-places and lastly, is the menu comprehensive? Don't be put off by the faded photographs of food outside the taverna, most are like this and if you were to stand outside in the sun all day you would fade too!

Service in most of the restaurants is good, if sometimes a little slow, especially when it comes to obtaining the bill, but remember you are on holiday, so relax. It is acceptable for you to ask to look at the food in the kitchen and enquire about any particular dish. You may feel a little wary at doing so, but whenever I have asked, they have been more than happy to show me around and answer any questions. If you fancy fish, ask if it is fresh, by law they have to specify this.

Most dishes come with French fries and/or rice and often with a small amount of salad. If you are partial to salad, it may be advisable to order an extra portion, beware though they are usually large, so one will be enough for two people.

If, after your main course you do not order a pudding, many tavernas will bring some melon, mousse, or honey cake on the house to thank you for your custom, or you will get a small glass of Ouzo or Metaxa with the bill. It is worth keeping an eye out to see what that particular taverna's approach is. One further point to remember is that in Greece the salt and pepper pots tend to be the opposite way round, i.e. the salt pot has multiple holes and the pepper a single hole.

Insider tip: *Beware of ordering UK branded spirits or unusual liqueurs without asking the price first. On my first trip to Kos I ordered a Glayva and almost had to take out a mortgage to pay for it!*

Most tavernas and restaurants are open all day serving breakfast, lunch and dinner. For those who want a more British start to the day, I'm afraid I'm one of those, a well-cooked and comprehensive English breakfast can be obtained at most tavernas, with only the bacon being a little different but still very tasty. The cost with juice, tea or coffee, the usual egg, bacon, sausage, beans, tomatoes and toast is around 6€. The alternative of a continental breakfast is always available.

Lunch, if you can manage it after breakfast, is invariably the same menu as that in the evenings, but most places do snacks and salads as an alternative.

In the towns and larger villages, there are a number of fastfood outlets, where you can eat in, or buy a take away such as a rotisserie chicken, kebab, or burger meal. In Kos Town there are two Italian restaurants and one Chinese.

Insider tip: *If you are not 'self-catering', hotel and apartment management tend to frown upon guests eating their own food in the rooms. I would also advise that where it is acceptable, it is courteous to dispose of any food waste yourself and not leave it for the hotel cleaning staff.*

A quick guide to Greek food

For those less familiar with Greek food, on the following pages I have outlined the main dishes you will find in the majority of tavernas (*in alphabetical order*).

Appetisers

Briam (*also a main course*) - Briam is an oven roasted vegetable dish that can be adapted according to what is in season. Layers of vegetables are baked in a savoury tomato sauce and served either as the main meal or as a tasty side dish.

Dolmades - Vine leaves stuffed with rice and then rolled. A hot variation also contains minced meat. Served most often cold as an appetiser, but can also be served hot with an avgolemono sauce on top. Its origin is thought to be from Thebes about the time of Alexander the Great.

Keftedes - Small rissoles or fritters, often made with minced lamb, pork or veal, onion, egg and herbs and sometimes with ouzo as a moistener. Keftedes are shaped into flattened balls and usually fried.

Mezes - A plate containing a selection of different appetisers, similar to the Spanish tapas, usually to be shared around the table. Mezes can include seafood, meats, vegetable dishes and dips.

Prawn Cocktail - Similar to the old style UK version with salad and cocktail sauce, but usually a very large portion.

Taramosalata - Greek caviar combined with breadcrumbs, oil, onion, and lemon juice to compliment any meal as an appetiser. This is a thick pink or white puree of fish roe (*dependent on the type of fish*).

Tzatziki - A yoghurt, cucumber and garlic dip to be served chilled on its own, or with pita or plain bread. Great on a Gyro.

Main courses

Grilled meats - Grilled meat usually includes lamb chops, pork, veal and chicken, either plain or in a variety of sauces dependent on the restaurant.

Gyro - Thin slices of barbecued meat specially seasoned with herbs and spices, served with tomatoes and onions on pita bread, and topped with tzatziki. Best from a rotisserie.

Kleftico or Klephtiko - Is a term that refers to any kind of meat dish that is sealed and baked. The word comes from the time of the Greek revolution, when bands of Greek guerrillas, called Klephts, hid in the mountains and cooked their dinner in pits sealed with mud, so that smoke and steam would not escape and betray their position. Usually it will be Lamb Kleftico that is on the menu.

Moussaka - A Greek national dish, Moussaka is prepared with sliced eggplant, lean ground beef, onions, tomatoes, butter, eggs, milk, cheese and seasonings and baked in an oven.

Omelette - Most tavernas offer a variety of omelettes on their menu.

Pasta - Spaghetti Bolognese is a firm favourite on most menus and usually very good. A wide range of other pasta dishes are also normally available.

Pastitsio - A Greek Lasagne combining macaroni, minced meat, cheese and covered with béchamel sauce.
Pilafi - Fluffy rice simmered in butter, spices and rich chicken stock.

Pizza - Where pizzas are concerned there are some tavernas that specialise, having the proper ovens and expertise. So my advice would be to ask around to find the best place to go, but personally I have found most are at least equivalent in quality to the best in the UK.

Roast Chicken - Both from an oven or a spit, cooked in olive oil. I personally think the rotisserie chickens are the best and taste as chicken should taste. Chicken in most restaurants on the island tends to be in fillet form. However, there are a few tavernas where you can still get a half chicken on the bone.

Roast Lamb - Lamb prepared in the traditional Greek way, roasted with herbs and olive oil.

Seafood - As with the majority of Mediterranean countries, in Greece you can find a wide variety of fresh and tasty seafood. I would suggest though that before ordering you ask if the fish is fresh and not frozen. Many restaurants and tavernas have a chilled fresh seafood cabinet near the entrance and the waiters are usually happy to confirm the choice of fresh fish they have on offer.

If you fancy splashing out on a lobster dinner, those restaurants that have fresh lobster on their menu usually require 24 hrs notice; I would also ask what the price would be per person and not per kilo. If you order prawns, the average price is around 10€ and you get about six, king-sized and in their shells.

Souvlaki - Souvlaki are made from cubes of meat that have been marinated for several hours in olive oil, lemon juice & origano, then threaded on wooden skewers and grilled or barbequed. They can be beef, veal, chicken, lamb, or pork.

Spanakopitta - Spanakopitta is a spinach pie, about the size of a flan. These small pies are made with a spinach and feta cheese filling in filo pastry. In Greek bakeries they are referred to as Spanakopittes, but don't be confused they can also be called Spanakotiropitakia.

Stamnato - Usually made with lamb (*often spelt lamp or lab!*) with potatoes in tomato and garlic sauce, baked in a traditional pot called a Lamm.

Stifado - Stifado is a casserole made of beef, veal or lamb in wine with pearl onions, tomatoes, herbs and spices.

Patisseries

Baklava - Nut filled, paper-thin layers of glazed filo pastry soaked in pure honey make this the king of pastry desserts. Every country in the near-east claims baklava is its own.

Diples - Honey rolls so thin and flaky that they crumble when they are bitten.

Halva - Is a candy made from ground sesame seeds. It is an oriental originated sweet, popular in Greece.

Kataifi - A delicious pastry made of shredded filo pastry rolled with nuts and honey and sprinkled with syrup. Found throughout the Mediterranean.

Koulouria - Also called Koulourakia - Breaded butter cookies with a light sugar glaze, perfect with coffee.

Kourabiedes - Sugar covered crescent shaped cakes that melt in your mouth. They are usually served at weddings, at Christmas, and on special occasions, such as birthdays and holidays.

Loukoumades - Feathery light honey tokens or sweet fritters, deep fried to a golden brown and dipped in boiling honey. A tasty delight from ancient Greece, where they were given as prizes to winners of athletic games.

Melomakarona - A honey cookie sprinkled with a spice-nut mixture.

Coffee

Greek style coffee - This is a thick, powdered coffee that is made in a brickee (*or brika*), which is traditionally a small brass pot with a long handle. Modern advances have given us stainless steel brikas. This is not instant coffee, and even though powdered, the coffee used does not dissolve. The grounds settle to the bottom of the cup.

When you order coffee of any sort, you must specify plain, sweet or medium-sweet (*sketo, glyko or metrio in Greek, respectively*). You can also order Cappuccino, Expresso and other types of coffee in most restaurants. Tea is usually available, but it comes in a do-it yourself style and can taste a little odd due to the long-life milk often used. I would recommend you ask for fresh milk.

Ouzeries

A traditional Greek style of eating out is at an Ouzerie, a blend of bar and taverna. Ouzeries usually only offer mezedes and possibly a few seasonal dishes, with (*if you want to be really Greek*) an Ouzo, Souma, or Retsina as an accompanying drink. Mezedes comprise a selection of small dishes or appetizers, placed around the table for you to pick and choose.

This is an easy and cost effective way to sample some traditional Greek food.

Shopping

Cigarettes, sweets and newspapers

In all the towns and resorts you will notice large wooden kiosks on the pavements of the main streets. This is where in Greece you traditionally buy such items as cigarettes and tobacco, newspapers, magazines, ice-cream, drinks, sweets and snacks such as crisps. The supermarkets also sell all of these except usually newspapers.

If you smoke and are visiting from an EU country, don't bother bringing any with you and remember Greece is in the EU, so you won't be able to purchase them in the duty free at your departure airport. Once in Greece you will find that they are vastly cheaper than back home, at a little less than 4€ for a packet of 20. You needn't shop around as the price will be the same at all the outlets. All the main UK brands are available such as Marlboro, Rothmans, Superkings, Benson & Hedges, etc. As Greece is in the EU, the rule banning smoking in any enclosed building also applies here. In summer though, most tavernas and bars are open-air and therefore you are free to indulge.

For those who become homesick whilst away and want to know what new stealth taxes the government have imposed, English newspapers are available, although they will sometimes be the previous day's edition. I have personally seen on sale The Daily Mail, The Mirror, The Sun and a couple of the main broadsheets, so you should have a good choice.

English magazines are rarer, but I have seen some of the main women's publications on the newsstands.

Men's clothes and shoes

As with most products on Kos, clothes and shoes are cheaper than in the UK. However, the selection of modern men's wear is not as good as for females, but there are some good fashion shops in the larger resorts. There is a reasonable selection of men's shoes although still limited, especially where fashion designs are concerned, but the prices are good and you may be able to pick up a real bargain.

Personal electronic items

I have yet to survey in detail the cost of personal electronic equipment, but my initial view is that it will be less expensive than in the UK and as Greece is in the European Union, it may be worth putting off that purchase and checking while you are over here. I will endeavour to check out this category of goods in the next month or so and add the results in the next update of this book.

However, it may be a problem if the goods turn out to be faulty. If you do intend to purchase expensive items, check first that the manufacturer's guarantee will cover the item back home.

Souvenirs

Well this is a difficult subject to write about as we all have a different view of what a good souvenir is. In all the resorts on the island there are a myriad of shops selling everything from quality items to the many explicit statues of well endowed male gods! Gold jewellery is good value as are leather goods and local pottery. If you really get stuck there is always a bottle of Ouzo, Metaxa or some local honey.

With regard to cosmetics, fashion, hairdressers and jewellery, I will pass this section over to my partner Carol.

Cosmetics

Although Kos is an island, as far as buying your moisturiser, body lotions, shampoos, make up etc and the all-important sunscreen you don't have to worry. Especially in the towns there is a good selection in the many pharmacies on the island and in some larger supermarkets. There are many known brands for sale but if yours is not available then there are equivalent Greek brands available at reasonable prices. In Kos Town there is also a large department store, the Hondas Centre that has an extensive range of perfumes, cosmetics and toiletries. So no need to waste valuable space and weight in your suitcase, just buy all you need when you arrive.

Fashion

Kos Town has an array of different shops to cater for every taste, from fun boutiques, to designer outlets. On my first visit I made the mistake of buying my holiday clothes in the UK only to find, there was so much more choice in Kos Town and a lot cheaper, with no compromise on quality. Beachwear, daywear and something special for a night out on the town can be found in the centre of Kos Town. You will find the designer/specialised clothes shops if you venture away from the centre down the many sides streets. Shoes and handbags are especially good value.

Hairdressers

There are numerous salons in Kos Town and most of the main resorts, and after a few days in the sun and sea, what better way to treat your hair, and yourself, than having a few hours relaxation and pampering, preparing for your evening out in one of the many clubs, restaurants and tavernas. I have had personal experience of one of the salons in Kos Town where I had an excellent shampoo, cut and blow dry for 30€ - extremely good value compared to UK prices!

Jewellery

It seems that nearly every shop you pass in Kos Town and the larger resorts sell some kind of jewellery - bangles, bracelets, rings, necklaces, earrings and much more. There is an amazing choice for every age and at modest prices. You could buy a different piece for each night of your holiday!

Again for more specialised jewellery and unique designs in Kos Town you will need to shop away from the centre. You may see something to treasure and keep as a memory and perhaps add to on your next visit.

Supermarkets

The supermarkets in the resorts and main towns are well provisioned for the UK holidaymaker. Many brands are recognisable and if not, the supermarket staff are usually very helpful. Milk comes in cartons, just look out for the Greek word γαλα (*Yala*), the required percentage and skinned or semi-skimmed. Crisps are known as chips in Greece and chips are known as French Fries, although supermarket and taverna staff are familiar with both terminologies.

If you want to eat in, supermarkets usually have a good selection of fresh vegetables and fruit on sale, but meat, other than the basics such as cooked cold meats and bacon have to be bought from the local butcher, just ask and they will tell you where it is.

There are takeaways in the main resorts with a good selection of fast food, also if you don't have the facilities to cook meat in your accommodation, many tavernas and restaurants, if you ask nicely, will do a takeaway service for main meat items such as a roast chicken.

If you want bread or pastries for later on in the day, I would advise you buy them early, as the supermarkets tend to sell out before lunchtime.

All the supermarkets sell wines and spirits, with again most of the brands we are used to in the UK available on the island. The selection of lagers is International, alternatively, the Greek lagers such as Fix and Mythos are in my view excellent. In addition to the supermarkets, there are usually dedicated off-licences in the main resorts that stock an even greater range. Prices are at least comparable with the UK, if not cheaper.

H.M. Customs

Regarding taking goods back home, if the goods you are carrying have had tax paid in Greece you do not have to pay any tax or duty on them in the UK. Any alcohol or tobacco you bring in must be for your own use and transported by you.

Own use includes goods for your own consumption and gifts. If you bring in goods for resale, or for any payment, even payment in kind, they are regarded as being for a commercial purpose.

With regards to quantities allowed, you are particularly likely to be asked questions by customs officers if you have more than:

800 cigarettes, 200 cigars, 400 cigarillos, 1 kg tobacco, 110 litres of beer, 90 litres of wine, 10 litres of spirits, 20 litres of fortified wine such as port or sherry.

Some goods are banned, such as plant materials that could contain diseases.

The information above is correct at the time of going to press.

With regard to buying honey as a souvenir or present, you may be told by some holiday reps that there are restrictions in taking it back into the UK. I have checked with H.M. Customs and DEFRA and as Greece is a member of the EU I can confirm there is no restriction.

Sports and recreation

Banana boats and ringos

For those not conversant with this activity, a banana boat is a long thin inflatable with seats for the participants positioned down its length. The banana is towed behind a speedboat and the objective is to stay on and enjoy the ride. Ringos are an alternative to the banana and are large inflatable rings towed behind the boat.

Banana and/or ringo rides can be found at all the main beaches. For safety's sake it is important that you wear the life jacket supplied.

Boat hire

Small outboard boats can be hired from some of the beaches on an hr/day basis. Larger sea going boats can be hired on the island on a daily or weekly basis.

Cinema

There are two cinemas on the island, namely Orfeas Summer and Orfeas Winter, both in Kos Town. Orfeas Summer is open-air and operates between June and October. There is a bar and snacks are available on site. Films usually change every few days and they have the latest titles in English.

Orfeas Winter is a traditional cinema with air-conditioning and is located in the centre of town.

Orfeas telephone number: 22420 25713

Cycling

The flat plains in the north have made cycling uniquely popular on Kos and there are some 5,000 cycles for hire at the height of the season.

Kos is also one of the few, if not the only island to have dedicated cycle lanes over much of the island. The only road that is busy is the one from Kos Town to Kefalos, all the others have little traffic and are safe for cycling. Bike hire is available in many places with prices from 4 to 12€ a day, cheaper if you hire for several days. Cycles come with locks so you needn't worry about security, but beware, they all look the same, so it's a good idea to tie something on it, so you can spot which one is yours.

Insider tip: Don't try to load a bike onto a local bus, they are not allowed.

Kos Mountain Bike in Kardamena, offer guided mountain bike tours (*25-80km*) from intermediate to advanced levels, as well as mountain bike hire. They provide quality mountain bikes (*Specialized Rockhoppers, 29ers and Camber full suspension*).

All bikes come with helmet, lock, pump, tube, map and 1.5 litres water, tel.: 6970 564 479

Fishing

Fishing is a popular pastime on the island for the locals, both by boat and off-shore, but for those visitors who would like to relax and try their luck with a rod and tackle, then most of the main resorts have a shop selling fishing tackle and bait.

It is often the local hardware retailer or similar, that doubles up as a fishing shop and although I am not an experienced fisherman, I have been surprised at the quality and range of gear on offer and the low cost of the items. To give an idea to the interested reader, a good extendable rod is around 15€.

The sea around the island abounds with a wide variety of fish, a fact that confirms the absence of pollution. The species include mullet, bream, blackfish, grey pandora, picarel and horse mackerel, with molluscs and crustaceans such as octopus and lobster.

Flyboarding

In 2013, Kos was the first Greek island to offer the new extreme sport of Flyboarding. The sport is water based and on Kos the centre offering the amazing sport is located on the beach 50 metres from the Oceanis Beach & Spa Resort in Psalidi. The centre has a team of trained and licensed instructors.

To explain the concept, the participant stands on the 'Flyboard' and is strapped on via boots. The board is attached to a Jet Ski by a Kevlar hose that pumps high pressure water through the base of the board allowing the 'flyer' to rise as high as ten metres in the air. By using their feet and additional water-jets strapped to the arms they can control the direction in which they 'fly', either though the air or underwater.

For details tel.: 6940110540

Go-Karting

Christos Go-Karts are situated between Tigaki and Marmari. This is the largest Go-Kart track on the island. A wide range of karts are available to suit all tastes and ages. For toddlers (*3 to 6 years of age*), there are small battery operated electric karts, which run on a specially created track, isolated from the main Go-Kart track for added safety. For young visitors (*6 to 9 years of age*) there are mini-karts available, all other ages can choose from standard 4-stroke karts or 2-stroke racing karts.

Opening hours are from 09:30 to 23:00 daily. Tel.: 22420 68184

GoKart Kardamena as the name implies is near Kardamena, located 7 km from the main square in the town. They even have two-seaters, so if one doesn't want to drive, they can still enjoy the fun.

The track is open from 11:00 until 23:00 every day. Tel.: 2242092065.

Horse riding

Horse riding is available on the island for all levels of competence, beware though when booking that it is a reputable company and is one that offers the type of riding that you require.

Alfa Horse, is a large riding stables based in the village of Amaniou (*situated between Zia and Pyli*) and has a good reputation as one of the quality stables on the island. However, I suggest you ask at your hotel/apartment who they recommend in your area.

Jet skis

Jet skis are available for hire on a number of beaches, these include Paradise, Kardamena and Kamari.

Paragliding

There is paragliding on most major beaches such as Paradise, Kardamena and Kamari. All the major companies supply safety equipment.

Pedaloes and Oxoon

Pedaloes are self-explanatory and are available on all the main beaches. Oxoon are a recent addition to Kos and are motorised, joystick steered 3-seat craft that look something like a dodgem car on the sea. Oxoon can be found at the water-sports centre at Kardamena as well as on other beaches.

Room Escape

In 2015, the new entertainment craze **Room Escape** arrived on Kos. Since its inception, this new concept has gone viral across the world. In Athens, it holds first place in TripAdvisor's list of the top attractions in the city, even taking first and second places above the Acropolis Museum (3rd) and the Temple of Hephaestus (4th).

Kos' Room Escape is based in the resort of Kardamina. The scenario of the attraction is that a group of 'players' (from 2 to 7) are locked in a room and they have to escape by solving puzzles to obtain the key....and all within a time of one hour!

There are two rooms to choose from, the 'Passage' and the 'Basement', with different storylines, namely a "murder" and a "kidnapping". All that players need is perception, observation and a spirit of cooperation to solve the mystery of the room and escape!

Tel: 6981718425

Spa and fitness

There are a number of the larger hotels on the island that have spas and gyms that are open to non-residents. My advice would be to ask locally where the nearest facilities are and check beforehand their availability and price.

Sub-aqua

There are five certified dive-centres on Kos, namely the Arian Diving at Kardamena, tel: 22420 92776, Kos Divers at the Padi Resort, Panorama Hotel, Kipriotis village, near Psalidi, tel: 22420 21553, Liamis Dive Centre, based in the Old Harbour, Kos Town, tel: 6944 295 830 and Sea Spirit Diving which have centres on Kardamena Beach and at the 5 star Kos Imperial Thalasso Hotel in Psalidi, tel: 6948334854.

Tennis, mini-golf, etc.

There are a vast array of other activities of the island, too many to mention here, such as tennis and mini-golf. My advice would be therefore to ask locally what is available in your resort.

Tenpin Bowling

Kos Town has a Tenpin Bowling alley with six professional lanes. There is a snack bar which also serves Chinese food. The alley is open from 16:00 until midnight.

Tel: 2242029132/3

Turkish Bath (*Hamam*)

If you participate in some of the other sports and entertainment in this chapter, a Turkish Bath may just be the perfect way for you to relax and unwind.

There is only one Hamam on Kos, namely The Artemis Hamam in Tigaki, which offers a wide range of traditional Hamam services.

The Hamam also has a bar where you can while away the evening listening to live music.

Open 09:00 till late, Tel.: 22420 67270

Watersports

There are a wide range of watersports available on most of the popular beaches on Kos. However, five of the main watersports centres on the island are at the Kos Imperial Hotel in Psalidi, Baywatch in Kefalos, Papas Beach Club on Milos Beach, Xtreme Watersports near Milos Beach, with the largest on the island being the Kardamena Watersports Centre, based at Kardamena.

The range of watersports available at each beach differ, but most include the main attractions of jetskis, windsurfing, water-skiing, canoeing, Oxoons, Ringos and Parascending.

Windsurfing

Windsurfing is available on many of the larger beaches and near Psalidi, there is the Big Blue Surf Centre in the Oceanis Hotel, where they specialise in teaching people to windsurf.

Tel: 2242021553.

Money matters

There are six main banks in Kos Town. These are branches of the National, Emporiki, Piraeus, Alpha, Dodecanese and Agricultural banks. In Kardamena there are branches of the Emporiki and National banks and in Kefalos and at the airport, there are branches of the Emporiki bank. These all have ATM machines, which take most debit and credit cards. Many stand-alone ATM's for the above banks are also situated within all the main resorts and in some major hotels.*

The charges for the use of your card will for the most part depend on your bank back home, so it might be wise to have a discussion with your bank/building society before you leave and confirm the costs you will incur. If you use one of the banks on the island to exchange Sterling or traveller's cheques, take your passport with you to the bank to confirm your identity.

Other than the banks, there are a wide choice of exchange options, many hotels, shops and car hire companies will also exchange Sterling, but make sure you check the rate and any charges first. Again the Greeks are very honest and I have never been short-changed, but it is advisable just to check.

In the banks, you may find a queue and remember life is at a slow pace in Greece. Look around as there may be a ticket-machine where you are required to take a numbered ticket identifying your place in the queue.

As to the exchange rate, I certainly have found that it is generally equal or better than that found back in the UK, so if you don't want the hassle of picking up currency before you leave home, just bring Sterling and change it on the island, for example in August 2013 the exchange rate in the UK was 1.22 on the island it was 1.24.

Credit/Debit cards are not accepted in many tavernas and smaller shops on the island, so it is advisable to carry sufficient money with you on days and evenings out. One further point regarding drawing cash out abroad via a credit card (*learnt from personal experience*), is that many card companies will not only charge you a relatively high exchange commission, but also an additional cash advance fee. So if you want to use your credit card abroad, I would therefore I advise you check on potential charges before leaving home.

With regard to the safety of carrying money and leaving it in your room, as I have stressed before, the Greeks are extremely honest and over the last 30 years of travelling in Greece, I have never had anything stolen. On the contrary, I have accidentally left valuable items in public places, only to find them untouched hours later, but remember, there are not only Greeks on the island!

At the time of going to press, currency exchange rates were unstable and therefore I have not included a reliable rate. However, the latest exchange rates and both Visa and MasterCard ATM* (*hole in the wall*) locators can be found on our website. At the top of the homepage click the 'Travel Club' tab, then 'Travel Club Kos' and finally 'Kos Travel Info'.

The bank opening hours are Monday to Friday: 08:00 - 14:00.

Insider tip: *If you are exchanging money, it is advisable to be at the bank well before 14:00.*

Phone numbers: (*Prefix for Kos - 22420, required for all calls*)

National Bank of Greece	:	22420 23317, 22420 28517
Emporiki Bank	:	22420 28825, 22420 22659
Agricultural Bank of Greece	:	22420 22226, 22420 28501
Alpha Bank	:	22420 28429, 22420 23486
Piraeus Bank	:	22420 28626, 22420 26097

Weather

What can you say about the weather in Greece other than it is invariably fabulous. To be more precise, what you would call summer back in the UK usually starts in May with temperatures rising throughout the following months (*see the table below*). Through late April, May and early June, and then again in October, the weather can be compared to a good British summer.

The months of July and August tend to be the hottest, with average daily temperatures ranging from 82°F (*28°C*) during the day to 72°F (*22°C*) at night. The high temperatures often spark off thunderstorms in the evening, but these are not usually accompanied by rain and are more entertaining than a nuisance.

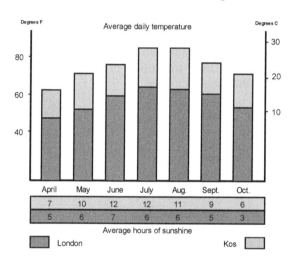

Rainfall is almost non-existent in summer, but showers can be expected between October and March.

The Meltemi

The Meltemi (*the Greek equivalent of the French Mistral*) is a powerful wind that blows across all of the Aegean islands. It is the result of a high-pressure system over the Balkans and a low-pressure system over Turkey, creating strong northeast winds. The

Meltemi occurs mainly during the summer with July and August being the worst affected months, but it can spring up occasionally in May and October. It usually starts in the early afternoon and can die out at sunset although occasionally, it will last through the night and repeat for three to six, sometimes even ten days. However, on Kos I have never found it a problem. Remember though not to leave valuables on the balcony, or you may return to find they've disappeared!

In September the evenings begin to cool, but that can be a blessing for those who enjoy a good night's sleep. Temperatures continue to drop into October and through to December and in January and February there can be the Kos winter, which is more like a UK spring.

The latest weather forecast can be found on our website by going to the 'Travel Club' tab, open the 'Kos' drop-down menu and go to 'Kos Weather'.

Bugs, biters and things

This chapter is not for the paranoid, as I have been true to my word, adding a definitive list of the bugs and biters on the island. However, that does not mean that any of the following are a threat to life and limb and I can confirm that regarding all listed, I have never met anyone who has suffered more than the usual mosquito bites or the very rare wasp sting, so with that in mind, the facts are:-

Ants

There are ants of course on the island and they remind me of the *Fire Ants* of the southern states of America. Leave any food out in easy reach and you may return to find a long procession of thousands of the critters offloading it back to their nest. It can be quite an entertainment, watching them manhandle something many times their size and never giving up.

Bees

Bees are less likely to sting than wasps, the reason being that the unlike the wasp, the bee stinger has barbs which prevents the insect withdrawing it. Brushing the bee off therefore results in the stinger and venom sack being ripped out of the insect, inevitably leading to its death.

Stingers should be scraped out sideways with a credit card, finger nail, or any sharp object. This helps to prevent squeezing the venom sack, which would lead to further venom being injected.

Treatment of the sting:-

1. Pull stinger out.
2. Cool compresses with ice.
3. Diphenhydramne (*Benadryl*) should be given to decrease minimal allergic reactions.
4. If a severe allergic reaction occurs, seek medical advice immediately.

Creams can be obtained from pharmacies to reduce the itching and inflammation.

Centipedes

Centipedes are not usually found in urban areas, they prefer rural and forested areas. Centipedes can bite humans, millipedes don't. The centipede's venom causes pain and swelling in the area of the bite, and may cause other reactions throughout the body. The majority of bites are not life-threatening to humans and present the greatest risk to children and those who develop allergic reactions. If bitten, consult a doctor or pharmacist at the earliest opportunity.

Hornets

There are hornets on Kos, but small numbers mean they are not a problem. They have a fearsome reputation for stinging and causing considerable harm, but in fact their stings are only a little more painful than that of a wasp or bee, due to the fact that hornet venom contains a larger amount (5%) of acetylcholine. Like most bees and wasps they usually only sting if you are blocking a flight path or are moving rapidly; however, nests should be avoided at all costs! For those that are not familiar with hornets, they have similar colouring to a wasp, being a member of the wasp family, but are about twice the size.

Horse Flies

Found throughout warmer climates, the Horse Fly is the largest of the fly species. Recognised by its size and a grey mottling on the back of the thorax, only the female fly bites, just prior to egg-laying. If you do get bitten, make sure the fly is either swatted or gone, as they can be persistent little critters, drinking blood from the wound. Treat any wound as you would a mosquito bite.

Jellyfish stings

If you do experience a sting, the quickest remedy is applying urine to the affected area, so pick your holiday companions carefully!

Mosquitoes

There is the usual problem of mosquitoes on the island, but a good covering of mosquito repellent in the evenings, sold at all supermarkets, should generally protect you. It does though seem to be dependent on the person, I rarely get bitten, whereas my partner Carol seems to attract all the little critters. Her answer is she has better quality blood!

I would advise you to use a mosquito machine in your bedroom, which can be the old plug-in heated tablet type (*the tablets are still available*), or the new heated liquid system. After testing the latter, they are in my view superior, one bottle of liquid should last for the whole holiday and there are no fiddly tablets to change every day.

Mosquito bites

Although there are over the counter remedies available at the local pharmacies, you could try applying vinegar to the bites and you will find the itchiness will subside.

Scorpions

Rarely seen, the species found on Kos is *Euscorpius Germanus*, also called the Small Wood-scorpion. As their common name implies, they are small at around 2 - 3cm in length and dark brown in colour. They tend to hide in crevices and such places as wood piles. In the most unlikely event that you are stung, the effect of the venom of this species is, for most people, no worse than a wasp sting.

Sea Urchins

As with beaches anywhere in the world, sea urchins can be found in some beach areas on the island. If you have children, a quick chat at one of the beach tavernas, or a scan for their remains on the beach will confirm whether to take precautions. If they are around the simplest solution is to wear swim shoes when entering the sea.

If you do step on one, consult a doctor or pharmacist and they will advise you on the best course of action. However, don't worry, it will usually mean nothing more serious than a little discomfort.

Here is the advice given in a medical journal:-

- Look for the signs and symptoms of a sea urchin sting: small spines embedded in the skin; a localized brownish-purple colour where the barbs made contact with the skin.
- Use sterile tweezers to remove any embedded spines.
- Control bleeding by applying direct pressure to the wound.
- Irrigate the wound with an irrigation syringe.
- Clean the wound with a disinfectant solution.
- Immerse the foot in hot water for at least 30 minutes, until pain subsides.
- Elevate the foot to control swelling.
- Dress the wound with a sterile bandage.
- Monitor for signs of infection. These signs include swelling, redness, pus, red lines radiating from the site of the wound, heat at the site of the wound, and fever.
- Seek medical advice.

Snakes

With regard to snakes, I have only seen one that was crossing the road and I saw it too late, it is now a flat-snake! There are a number of species on the island as in all of Greece, but only one is poisonous, namely the Viper. Most vipers are nocturnal and are only sporadically observed in the daylight, when they bask or mate. It is easy to distinguish a viper from the harmless species, based on their triangular head, swollen cheeks, stout body and a zig-zag pattern running down their back (*vipers are seldom longer than one metre*). A viper bite is not necessarily poisonous, in only about 30%

of bites there is actual injection of venom, and thus a need for anti-venom treatment.

The rule is if you see a snake, be on the safe-side and leave it well alone, but *please* be assured, it is extremely rare to hear of a bite. The precautions that can be taken are that when out walking in long grass, wear ankle length boots and do not turn large stones over, or place your hand into crevices that might be home to a snake. If you were to be the *one in a million* and are bitten, the advice is to be safe and seek medical help straight away.

Wasps

A more irritating insect can be the wasp. They tend to be found in greater numbers near the populated beaches where there is a good supply of tourist food, with the areas around towns and villages having very few if any. So it is dependent on where you are and what you are doing. I can honestly say don't worry, the locals don't, just try to ignore them. I certainly haven't been stung in five years of living in Greece and just find them irritating at times. Another answer is to buy a fly swat and see how many you can exterminate. Sorry, I apologise to the entomologists amongst you.

If you find them irritating when you eating in a restaurant, ask the waiter for a "burner", usually a metal container filled with smouldering Greek coffee. The fumes are surprisingly an excellent deterrent to the little blighters. The good news is that come sundown they all return to their nest.

If you are unfortunate enough to get stung, the cheapest and quickest solution is to simply apply vinegar to the affected area. However, if you are allergic to stings, seek medical advice as soon as possible.

Creams to reduce the inflammation and itching can be purchased from pharmacies.

Health and Safety

Hospitals, doctors & community clinics

Whereas we all hope that nothing untoward happens on our holidays, especially health wise, as I can personally testify it sometimes does.

My view of the islands facilities is a good one, with all but the most serious incidents catered for on the island itself. In Kos Town there is a General Hospital, well equipped and easy to find by following the signs in the town. There are also private doctors in Kos Town and most of the resorts. Normally the surgery is near the middle of the village or resort centre and can be recognised by a red cross on the door, or on a sign in front of the building.

There are twelve pharmacies in Kos Town and at least one in each of the resorts. They operate on regular business hours (*usually 08:00 - 13:00 and 18:00 - 24:00*). One pharmacy in Kos Town stays open during the night and the early morning hours. As this is organised on a rota system, you need to check locally for details. You can also be assured the quality of medicines and advice is equal to that back home.

For emergencies there is a twenty-four hour doctor service at the General Hospital in Kos Town. Alternatively there are private doctors you can visit if the need arises.

Remember, if you are an EU citizen, you should apply for a European Health Insurance Card (*EHIC*), now designated the A1 card. This will allow you to obtain free or reduced cost treatment abroad; this includes only treatment provided on the state scheme. The EHIC is free of charge and can be obtained within the UK in the following ways. I advise that you apply well in advance of your trip, as it can take a week or two for the card to arrive:

By internet at **www.ehic.org.uk**
By telephone on 08456062030
Or by form from the Post Office
(*For other EU citizens, search the web by entering EHIC*)

Dental services

My own personal experience of ill health in Greece was in 2006, prior to moving to the island of Thassos to live. Only hours after arriving on the island, I was stricken by severe toothache and although I suffered for two further days (*I'm a man*), in the end I had to ask for help and was recommended to a dentist in Thassos Town.

All I can say is that I was amazed at the care shown to me on my arrival and the quality of the subsequent treatment. The surgery was modern, comfortable and very well equipped and the dentist friendly, he spoke fluent English and his chair-side manner was highly professional. I also found on my return to the UK, that the charges I had paid were less than half that I would have paid at home. All in all, I have to say that if I required dental work, I would prefer to have it done in Greece!

Contact details:

Kos General Hospital,
Mitropoleos and Ippokratous Streets,
Kos Town.
Telephone: 22420 28050, Ambulance: 22420 22300

Emergency services, telephone: 112

Emergency Police:

Telephone: 22420 22100

Doctors phone numbers:

Kardamena	: 22420 91202
Antimachia	: 22420 51230
Asfendiou	: 22420 69202
Kefalos	: 22420 71230
Pyli	: 22420 41230

Stomach upset

If the worst happens, try adding a little fresh lemon juice to a Greek coffee and knock it back and in no time at all the symptoms will ease.

Sunburn

The most obvious advice anyone can give is to be extra careful for at least the first few days! If like most, you are not used to the Mediterranean sun, take it very easy and use plenty of high factor sun-block cream. You are especially vulnerable when there is a breeze, or when you are travelling in an open top car, a point I learnt from bitter experience, as you do not feel the full extent of your skin's reaction to the sun.

If the worst does happen, my first advice is to visit the local pharmacy and seek help. If this is not possible, a cold shower will initially relieve the pain, but drip dry, as using a towel will only aggravate the situation. For mild sunburn, cool compresses with equal parts of milk and water may suffice. Another remedy, recommended by many, is to spray or pat the affected areas with white or cider vinegar; this will relieve the pain and itching and hopefully give you a good night's sleep until you can visit a pharmacy.

The symptoms may also be relieved by taking aspirin or ibuprofen, but do not exceed the doses specified on the label.

Safety

Where safety is concerned, the subject falls into two categories.

First there is the safety aspect with regard to crime; one of the points that has always attracted me to Greece, especially the islands, is the lack of both property and personal crime. It does exist, or there wouldn't be police or prisons in Greece, but as far as the tourist is concerned it is rare on Kos. What property crime does exist tends to be from the less desirable tourists and criminals from the poorer states near to Greece. If you see the police on the island they will usually be drinking coffee or chatting to colleagues. But be warned, if you do transgress the rules, the police can be quite heavy handed.

The advice is of course be careful, however, I have accidentally left expensive items in public places in the past, only to return many hours later to find them just where I left them.

With regard to valuable items and money left in your accommodation, again I have never heard of any problems. The room cleaning staff, I have met in the past, have proved totally honest and as long as you lock the windows and doors you should have no need to worry. Sadly there have been a few incidents of cars being broken into, especially when the owners leave valuables on show. So the rule is when you leave the car, put valuables in the boot and it is also worthwhile leaving the glove compartment open and empty.

In the event of a loss of a valuable item, remember that if you are insured, your insurance company will need written confirmation that the loss was reported to the local police.

The second category is safety with respect to the activities you participate in during your stay. Safety in Greece is less stringently policed than in the UK, so when you are out and about, and especially with children, extra care should be taken. To give an example, the railings around the battlements of the Knight's Castle are well below the quality we would expect to find in the UK.

Being abroad you should also take extra care when driving. Although the Greeks are mostly good drivers, compared to say the Italians, there does seem to be an unofficial rule that many follow, to the effect that they should not purely concentrate on driving their vehicle. Mobile phones, eating and drinking and even doing paperwork should all be a part of the driving experience!

Keep in mind though that if *you* are not experienced at driving on the right, mistakes can easily be made. It is a sobering sight on your travels, to see so many memorial boxes by the side of the road, especially by the cliff roads around the island.

As far as scooters and motorbikes are concerned, these are the most dangerous modes of transport on the island. You will see these being driven correctly with the riders wearing crash helmets, but usually only with shorts and T-shirts being worn and I have seen the damage tarmac and gravel can do to human flesh, even at slow speeds!

One further point is not to trust the zebra crossings, in Greece these mean little although the rules do give the pedestrian the right of way.

On the beach

If you have young children, just be a little careful on the beaches, as the currents can dredge out small holes in the seabed. This can be a shock to a child who finds that one minute they are in water a foot deep and the next up to their necks.

Swimming shoes

A recommended purchase is a pair of swimming shoes. They slip on and have a rubberised sole to protect you against sharp rocks and sea-urchins. They can be purchased at most beach-shops and cost around 8€.

Tony Oswin

Hints and tips

Batteries

All the usual UK battery sizes are available in the supermarkets at equivalent or cheaper prices than back home, but make sure you bring the battery chargers for your mobile phone, pda, etc.

Currency conversion

At the time of going to press, currency exchange rates were unstable and therefore I have not included a reliable rate in this edition. However, the latest exchange rates can be found on our website, www.atoz-guides.com

Distance conversion

1 mile = 1.61 kilometres

Electricity

The electricity on Kos and throughout Greece is 220V. You can purchase the two pin adaptors at the local electricity shops. So if you do not already own one, it may be cheaper to purchase them on the island.

Electric razors

Some accommodation of the island have dedicated razor points in the bathrooms, but if not the adaptors sold on the island will take a twin pin razor plug.

Embassies

UK - telephone: 22420 21549
Italy - telephone: 22420 21991
Sweden - telephone: 22420 26278
Finland - telephone: 22420 22340
Denmark - telephone: 22420 23301

Fire prevention

In the summer months, the vegetation on the island becomes parched and tinder dry. In the past the island has been ravaged by bush and forest fires and therefore it is essential to be careful, especially with discarded cigarettes. It is a strictly enforced law on the island that barbeques and camp fires are banned outside the town areas during the summer months.

Google Earth

For those with web access, an interesting and informative site is:-

www.earth.google.com

Here you can view satellite images of Kos. You will need to download the free basic version software, but it is well worth it. For quick access to satellite images of Kos, add the following coordinates into the top left-hand corner box and press search. This will take you to Kos Town.

36 53 40.20N 27 18 19.42E

Google Street View

In the last few years, the Google map car has been collecting data and photographs across the Greece to add the country to those already covered by their 'Google Street Maps'. For Kos, the main towns and tourist sites are now covered, To view 'Street Views', you need to enter 'Google Earth' and drag the orange man icon (*at the top right-hand side of the screen*) to the desired area.

Hair dryers

Many of the higher quality hotels and apartments supply a hairdryer in the room. If important, it is advisable to check with your tour-company or hotel before leaving home.

Internet connections

Most hotels offer WiFi facilities to guests with their own laptops, tablets or smartphones and larger hotels usually have an Internet room. In the main towns and resorts on the island many of the bars and cafés now also offer free WiFi to their customers. Alternatively, tourist resorts usually have at least one Internet café, with the cost being around 3€ an hour, making it a cost effective way of contacting home and retrieving your emails. Remember though to take your important email addresses with you!

Kos Airport

Sadly this information will only be of interest when you are returning home. However, the facilities are modern and as comfortable as any departure area. Once you pass through passport control, there are toilets, a café supplying drinks, snacks and chocolates and a small duty-free shop selling the usual cigarettes, booze and a selection of those last-minute present ideas.

Telephone: 22420 51229, 22420 56000

Mobile phones

Many mobile phone companies now offer reduced cost call packages for when you are abroad, but you will have to contact them and enquire what offers are available at the time of your trip. Also remember to get your phone unblocked for international calls before you leave home.

Police

There are police stations in nearly every large village or town. You will recognize the police station by the Greek flag flying from the building and of course by the police vehicles parked outside.

On Kos there is also a tourist police service (*Touristiki Astinomia*) for more holiday related problems. You will find the office of the tourist police in the same building as the island police in Kos Town, directly on the harbour front.

The tourist police also supply information and brochures on the island and help in searching for accommodation.

Tourist police office Kos Town, tel: 22420 26666

Post

As it is a tradition with us Brits to send home the usual wish you were here cards, I will cover posting on the island, but remember even if you post your cards soon after your arrival, it is highly likely you will be home before your cards!

The cost of the postcards and the stamps required for the UK is very low and you can purchase both in the supermarkets.

The Greek postal service is ELTA and post offices can be found in all the larger towns and are usually open from 07:30 to 14:00. Post boxes are coloured bright yellow and the post-office signs are yellow and blue.

Spelling

On your travels and in printed material, such as signs and menus, you will see names and places spelt in a variety of different ways. Do not be put off by the spelling, especially when you are trying to find somewhere, if it sounds the same, it probably is.

Sunbeds and parasols

If you are going to be a regular visit to the beach, rather than hire a parasol at an average of about 2.50€ a day, it may be cost-effective to buy one from one of the beachside supermarkets (*between 10 and 15€*). If you don't have a car and you are put off at the thought of carrying it back to your accommodation each day, you can ask nicely at the supermarket where you purchased it and they may allow you to leave it there overnight.

The same goes with the sunbeds; a good lilo can be purchased for around 10€ and gives you the added advantage of being able to use it in the sea, whereas a sunbed costs between 2 and 4€ each day. Many supermarkets have a compressor that they may allow you to use, so you can deflate it at the end of the day and take it back to your accommodation, or as before, ask nicely at the supermarket and they may allow you to leave it there.

Telephoning

Many apartments and hotels now have phones in the room; however, the cost of phoning home can be considerable. Alternatively many main landline providers in the UK, as well as independent telephone prefix companies, offer very low cost or even free international calls to Greece. It may therefore be cost effective to text relatives with your room telephone number and ask them to phone you. Remember Greece is 2 hours ahead of UK time.

Public telephones are to be found throughout the island, but remember, even in this age of mobile phones, there can be a queue of holidaymakers waiting to phone home, especially in resorts in the early evening.

To phone the UK the prefix is 0044 and you drop the first zero of the UK number, i.e. a London number that starts 020..... would translate into 0044 20....

To phone Greece from the UK and elsewhere, the prefix is 0030 and the prefix for Kos is 22420 (*the latter is required for all calls*).

One further option for phoning home is to use Skype, although a number of the Internet Cafes have Skype loaded, it is best to bring a headset or Skype phone with you, as not all cafes supply them. If you are familiar with Skype, you will know that phone calls home will only cost cents, compared with euro with alternative services.

Tipping

Tipping is an awkward subject to cover as it is obviously dependent on the quality of service you have received and at your personal discretion. The service you will receive on Kos is usually very good and if you take an average price for a meal for two of 30€, a tip of 10 - 15% is not excessive and quite acceptable. The local wages are low and it may also be courteous and prudent to tip within these limits.

Toilet paper

Next a delicate subject, but an important one. Due to the small bore of waste pipes that are used in Greece, it is a rule that toilet paper is not flushed, but deposited in the bin by the toilet. Although this can be a little embarrassing for some, it is better than having to call on the manager of your accommodation to help unblock the toilet. Don't worry though, the bins are emptied on a daily basis and shouldn't cause a problem.

Water

The tap water on Kos is drinkable, as the island is self sufficient in fresh water. If you do have a preference for bottled water you can find it at all supermarkets, restaurants, cafeterias and kiosks.

Telephone numbers

Emergency: 112

Emergency Police: 22420 22100
Tourist Police: 22420 26666
Ambulance: 22420 22300
Kos Hospital: 22420 28050 or 23423
Fire Department: 22420 22199
Tourist information: 22420 24460
Taxi station: 22420 22777
Bus station: 22420 26276
Port Police: 22420 26594

Zebra crossings

One further point to remember is not to trust the zebra crossings, in Greece these mean little although the rules do give the pedestrian "the right of way".

For the very latest tips and information, please visit our website at:-

www.atoz-guides.com

Tony Oswin

Glossary of Greek words and phrases

Below, I have included a few useful words with their Greek counterparts. Although the majority of Greeks on the island speak some level of English, with many being fluent, I have found that the Koans really appreciate visitors attempting their language, even if you make a proverbial "pig's ear" of it!

Yes	Nay
No	Orhee
Good morning	Kalimaira
Good afternoon/evening	Kalispaira
Please	Parakalo
Thank you	Efkaristo
No, thank you	Okhee efkaristo
The bill please	To logargiasmo parakalo, or simply make a gesture in the air as though you were signing your name.....it works!
Hello/Goodbye (*singular/informal*)	Yiassou
Hello/Goodbye (*plural/formal*)	Yiassas
How much	Poso kani
Coffee	Kafé
Tea	Chy
OK	Endaksi

Where is	Pooh eenai
Do you speak English	Meelahteh ahnggleekah
I don't understand	Dhehn kahtahlahvehno
Can I have	Boro nah ehkho
Can we have	Boroomeh nah ehkhoomeh
I'd like	Thah eethehlah
Tomorrow	Avrio
Today	Seemaira
Toilets	To tooalettes
Wine	Krassi
Good	Kahloss
Bad	Kahkoss
Bank	Trapeeza
Police	Astinomeea
Doctor	Yatdros
Now	Tora
What is the time	Ti ora ine
Cheers	Yammas
Sorry/excuse me	Signomee

Map of Kos Town

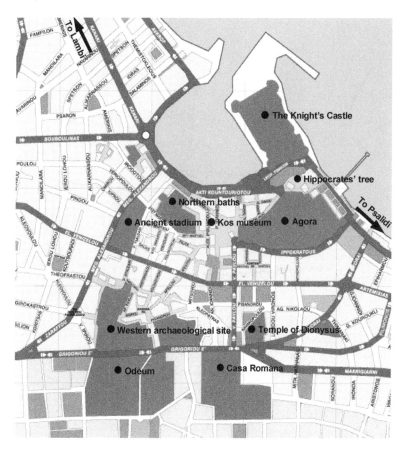

Map of the Asklepion

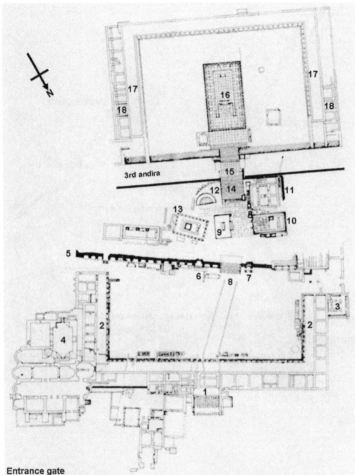

Entrance gate
1. Propylon (monumental gateway)
2. Hellenistic stoa
3. Ancient latrines
4. Roman Thermae (Baths)
5. Retaining wall
6. Springs
7. Small Temple dedicated to Nero
8. Staircase to the second andira
9. Altar (4th c. B.C.)

10. Ionic Temple of Asklepios (3rd c. B.C.)
11. Priests residence or Abaton
12. Semi-circular exedra
13. Corinthian Temple
14. Staircase to the third andira
15. Staircase to the fourth andira
16. Doric Temple of Asklepios (4th c. B.C.)
17. Stoa
18. Patients' dormitories

Map of Bodrum

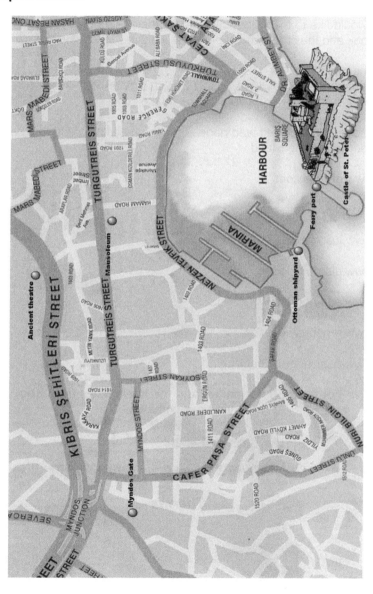

Acknowledgements and web sites of interest:

I would like to thank the following for their help in the writing of this book and the creation of the 'A to Z' website.

The people of Kos
Sonay Ercakalli, Turkish Tourist Board, London
Design & Digital Creative by www.verkko.co.uk

I have also included web pages that you may find of interest before your visit to the island.

www.greeka.com

www.hippocrates.gr

www.justkos.co.uk

www.discoverbodrum.com

www.alfa-horse.de

www.grecotel.com/kos

www.oasisbodrum.com

For further information and the latest news from Kos, visit our website:-

www.atoz-guides.com

Your 'A to Z Travel Club' password:-

Therma

2016

January

S	M	T	W	T	F	S
					1	2
3	4	5	6	7	8	9
10	11	12	13	14	15	16
17	18	19	20	21	22	23
24	25	26	27	28	29	30
31						

February

S	M	T	W	T	F	S
	1	2	3	4	5	6
7	8	9	10	11	12	13
14	15	16	17	18	19	20
21	22	23	24	25	26	27
28	29					

March

S	M	T	W	T	F	S
		1	2	3	4	5
6	7	8	9	10	11	12
13	14	15	16	17	18	19
20	21	22	23	24	25	26
27	28	29	30	31		

April

S	M	T	W	T	F	S
					1	2
3	4	5	6	7	8	9
10	11	12	13	14	15	16
17	18	19	20	21	22	23
24	25	26	27	28	29	30

May

S	M	T	W	T	F	S
1	2	3	4	5	6	7
8	9	10	11	12	13	14
15	16	17	18	19	20	21
22	23	24	25	26	27	28
29	30	31				

June

S	M	T	W	T	F	S
			1	2	3	4
5	6	7	8	9	10	11
12	13	14	15	16	17	18
19	20	21	22	23	24	25
26	27	28	29	30		

July

S	M	T	W	T	F	S
					1	2
3	4	5	6	7	8	9
10	11	12	13	14	15	16
17	18	19	20	21	22	23
24	25	26	27	28	29	30
31						

August

S	M	T	W	T	F	S
	1	2	3	4	5	6
7	8	9	10	11	12	13
14	15	16	17	18	19	20
21	22	23	24	25	26	27
28	29	30	31			

September

S	M	T	W	T	F	S
				1	2	3
4	5	6	7	8	9	10
11	12	13	14	15	16	17
18	19	20	21	22	23	24
25	26	27	28	29	30	

October

S	M	T	W	T	F	S
						1
2	3	4	5	6	7	8
9	10	11	12	13	14	15
16	17	18	19	20	21	22
23	24	25	26	27	28	29
30	31					

November

S	M	T	W	T	F	S
		1	2	3	4	5
6	7	8	9	10	11	12
13	14	15	16	17	18	19
20	21	22	23	24	25	26
27	28	29	30			

December

S	M	T	W	T	F	S
				1	2	3
4	5	6	7	8	9	10
11	12	13	14	15	16	17
18	19	20	21	22	23	24
25	26	27	28	29	30	31

Notepad